Chamfort

Chamfort

Reflections
on Life, Love
& Society

together with

Anecdotes and Little

Philosophical Dialogues

Selected, Translated and with
an Introduction by

DOUGLAS PARMÉE

✳ SHORT BOOKS

First published in 2003 by
Short Books
15 Highbury Terrace
London N5 1UP

10 9 8 7 6 5 4 3 2 1

A CIP catalogue record for this book
is available from the British Library.

ISBN 1-904095-62-3

Printed in Great Britain by
St Edmundsbury Press Ltd, Bury St Edmunds, Suffolk.
Jacket printed by White Quill Press Ltd, Croydon

Be a philosopher;
but amidst all your philosophy,
be still a man.

DAVID HUME

In place of fundamental truths I put
fundamental probabilities, provisionally
assumed guides by which
one lives and thinks.

FRIEDRICH NIETZSCHE

DEDICATION AND ACKNOWLEDGEMENTS

For the publication of this Selection, I wish to acknowledge inspiration and help from many kind people, too numerous to mention all by name. It is thus dedicated to all admirers of Chamfort – past, present and future. I must nonetheless name their current doyen Jacques Barzun, the loving biographer of Hector Berlioz and author of the monumental work *From Dawn To Decadence*.

I should also like to offer my thanks to the eminent Flaubertian and francophile novelist and critic Julian Barnes; and I owe a special debt to the friendly enthusiasms of Alain de Botton, Proustian, devotee of Chamfort, and the widely acclaimed author of *The Consolations of Philosophy*.

I owe my warmest thanks to my son Nick, himself a keen Chamfortian, for invaluable suggestions and unfailing goodwill; and to Sally Ling for her steadfast help.

I pay unlimited tribute to my wife Meg, who would have reduced Chamfort's wary, dubious misogyny effortlessly to dust.

Lastly, I feel privileged to have the good fortune to be the messenger of these reflections on Wisdom and Folly, the drug-free anti-depressant, continually provoking thought and frequently raising chuckles, in a word, teaching us how best to live, by Nicolas-Sébastien Roch de Chamfort.

D.P.

CONTENTS

**The glossary provides a basic introduction to all the
characters mentioned in the book
**This section contains endnotes, numbered
throughout the text*

INTRODUCTION

Chamfort was born in 1740 with an Achilles' heel: he was illegitimate. Hushed up at the time – his father a canon of the cathedral in what is now Clermont-Ferrand, his mother a member of the provincial nobility – the truth was always likely to come out and inevitably did. 'Canon' is a modest rank; Chamfort could not expect the flying start in life that might be the lot of sons of bishops, archbishops, cardinals or popes, and, more gallingly, he could not hope to benefit from the many privileges generally accruing to a man of his at least semi-noble birth: powerful connections, even with the Court itself; freedom from many taxes; access to the upper ranks of the army, navy or Church (closed shops for commoners) and general prestige – commoners' reverence for nobility might well allow an idle aristocrat to live, in style, on his debts (cf. Reflection No. 422). Chamfort had to create his own success; disadvantaged by being too proud to accept help from someone who was not a true friend or sincere admirer, his interest in philosophy or literature was unlikely to be lucrative, particularly as he showed no great talent in his chosen field of drama. His wit made him welcome, but in a society which his refusal to compromise led him to despise, how could he ever hope his life to be anything but precarious?

Things might have been worse. His adoptive parents were caring and he soon proved himself a very bright boy. When quite young (the exact age is uncertain, for his life still contains much undiscovered territory), he won a bursary to an excellent religious boarding school in Paris. Discipline was very strict; Chamfort must have resented the use of expert whippers to discourage the unruly as well as to drive out the Devil. On one occasion he ran away, but having reached Cherbourg, intending to take ship to the New World, seen at that time (except by black slaves) as the Promised Land of freedom and prosperity, he is reported as saying to a fellow fugitive: 'Before exploring the world, why not explore ourselves?' They went back and, amazingly, Chamfort settled down and became the school's most brilliant pupil, winning prize after prize and crowning his school career by coming first in the prestigious Concours Général, a competition open to all the schools of Paris and Versailles.

When he left school, he could justifiably claim to be the most eminent student of his year in the whole of France. On graduating, he also automatically acquired the title of abbé, a lay cleric, and could move effortlessly into the priesthood, a well-trodden path, especially for young men without financial or family backing, to a secure, respectable and, if you were so inclined, undemanding career. When his headmaster suggested this course, Chamfort made the typically frank, witty and biting reply of the kind which was later to be the joy of many eager listeners in Paris salons and fashionable cafés: 'I'd never become a priest; I'm too fond of peace and quiet, philosophy and women, honour and true fame and not fond enough of squabbling, hypocrisy, honours and money.' He gave up his title of abbé and created a grander pseudonym, rather bogus but in tune with current snobberies: Nicolas-Sébastien Roch de Chamfort. On his mother's side, the aristocratic 'de' was at least half-justified; but more significantly it was an assertion, by a man conscious of his intellectual superiority, of his ambition to make his way in a blatantly unjust society, in defiance of social and financial disadvantages: an arrogant shake of the fist at the world he intended to conquer. Later, to our great benefit, we find him assuming a far more entertaining pseudonym: the M... of his 'Reflections and Anecdotes', a man of considerable wit and outspoken integrity, largely represents Chamfort, at times an idealised Chamfort, one he would have liked to have been, a side of himself he preferred to express surreptitiously.

The studious boy turned into a studious and very widely-read man, for which he had excellent tools: Latin and Greek as well as Italian and, most importantly, English. His 'Reflections' contain quotations from or allusions to moralists of many cultures: the epicurean Lucretius, the stoic Seneca, the Christian Dante as well as the anti-Christian satirist Lucian, and, inevitably, the Cynic Diogenes; his work is spattered with mythological references, and we know that he translated from the Latin satirist Martial as well as the Greek Anthology[1]. He had great respect for many English works, sharing the disdain for make-believe and people *en masse* expressed by Francis Bacon and Swift, aspiring to the fluency and concision of Pope, admiring the thinking of Locke and questioning the paradoxes of Mandeville first-hand. He had extensive knowledge of French writers, from the early humanism of Rabelais, whose coarseness he deplored, to the later, subtler Montaigne. He was, naturally, very familiar with the writers of the *Grand Siècle*, particularly the moralists; he venerated the tragic dramatist Racine, whose grand style he was, tragically for himself, to emulate. He persistently and successfully pursued, for the sake of his literary aspirations, and always with one eye on election to the French Academy, the financially unrewarding prizes offered by various provincial academies for discourses on set moral or literary topics. Two notable successes were a *Eulogy of Molière*, in which, not unexpectedly, he concentrates on his subject's amused portrayal, in *Le Misanthrope*, of a stubbornly honest man who despises the insincerity of society while in love, to his embarrassment and our amusement, with a society woman; and on Molière's exposure of religious hypocrisy in *Tartuffe*. In 1769 it won him a prize from the French Academy itself, and in 1774, a *Eulogy of La Fontaine* (La Fontaine being as mischievous and charming a pricker of pretentious bubbles as Chamfort himself, and almost certainly as voluptuary) won the first prize from the prestigious Academy of Marseilles.

These successes lay ahead; Chamfort had meanwhile to learn the hard lesson that book-learning will not provide a living. He chose the usual options: hack work such as composing sermons for priests happy to deliver the fruits of another's labours; odd bits of journalism; and, inevitably, private tutoring, not, it appears, with great success: in one job, he seemed happier spending time with the pupil's mother than with her son; in another, more time with the female domestic staff than with his pupil; and in yet another, which took him to Germany, he quarrelled with his pupil's uncle. This tutoring is memorable mainly for his reported comment, on his return to France, that he knew no one less suited to be a German than himself. But backed by his academic record, he was able, in the sixties, to obtain more appropriate employment, collaborating on a reputable publication, the *Journal Encyclopédique*, and, later, on an important dictionary, the *Grand Vocabulaire Français*. It was an age eager to disseminate knowledge, and it was such tasks which, in combination with his reputation as an interesting character with a rather acerbic wit, finally brought him into the centre of intellectual activity of the century: the circle of writers and thinkers connected with the *Encyclopédie*. This work, launched in 1751 by Diderot and the mathematician d'Alembert, whom Chamfort came to know well, was a monumental attempt to classify systematically all available knowledge – an idea already mooted by Francis Bacon, whose writings Chamfort greatly admired: it was an attempt to give a rational, scientific explanation of the universe and thereby find truth and expose and destroy superstition. Its contributors included most of the leading writers and thinkers of the age: Voltaire, Rousseau, Montesquieu and many others, several of whom we shall find mentioned in Chamfort's 'Reflections' and many of whom he knew personally. He was, however, deeply sceptical of their excessive reliance on reason, knowing from personal experience that man is far from being a strictly rational creature and that achieving happiness by avoidance of pain and anxiety, which an epicurean considered the prime aim of life, was inadequate, undesirable, and, indeed, impossible by the use of reason alone.

Chamfort was fortunate to find amongst his *encyclopédiste* friends one who shared this scepticism: Pierre Duclos. More than thirty years his senior and one of the most influential intellectuals of his day, he took Chamfort under his wing: as permanent secretary of the French Academy, he was in a position to hold the balance between avant-garde and reaction, while as the royal historiographer he had access to Court circles. Through him Chamfort could achieve entry into any salon which he would want to frequent, and it was in those salons that reputations were to be made – and lost. Chamfort flourished in this stimulating atmosphere, where his breadth of reading, his sparkling, often biting wit, as well as his good looks, made him greatly prized by hostesses. He was particularly attached to the Helvétius salon, run by a charming and beautiful woman (who was to be very helpful to him in his later, more difficult years) and financed by her husband, a former Farmer-General[2], who, having acquired great wealth through this post, had retired to support the cause of the *philosophes*[3]. In his best-known work, *De l'Esprit*, one of the central texts of Enlightenment political thought, Helvétius argued that, since seeking pleasure is the mainspring of man's conduct, a government's main task is to ensure the greatest good for the greatest number – an idea which greatly influenced all future political thought, including the Utilitarian Jeremy Bentham, as well as the USA Constitution; a similar thread runs through many of Chamfort's own ideas about government and society.

In the elegantly easy-going ethos of the day, salon life gave full scope to Chamfort's liking for women; he was well-built as well as handsome – one of his lovers described him as not only an Adonis but also a Hercules. However, libertinism can often pall and Chamfort was still hungry for 'true fame', which he felt was to be found most surely in the theatre: in this age of spectacle, theatre-going – to be seen as well as to see – was one of the most popular forms of social activity, while in the salons themselves amateur theatricals competed with gambling for entertainment, for those occasions when conversation and flirtation were flagging.

His first theatrical venture was a one-act play in verse (an already outmoded genre), *La Jeune indienne*, which Chamfort succeeded in putting on stage in 1764. Despite the King's presence at one performance, its success was brief and unrewarding, both for his reputation and his finances. Voltaire read and said he liked it; the critics slated it; Rousseau admired it, for the theme was close to his heart and, indeed, somewhat prophetic for Chamfort's later social attitude. The *jeune indienne*, apparently from the Caribbean, is a child of nature – a noble savage – shocked to discover that a bride had to bring more than virtue and beauty to the marriage bed: so-called civilised society also demanded a hefty dowry.

Disappointed but undaunted, and doubtless encouraged by the success of the play in Berlin, Moscow and elsewhere abroad, where French culture enjoyed great prestige, Chamfort, after a few minor excursions into writing libretti for the currently very popular ballet-opera, tried ordinary theatre again in 1770, this time a prose comedy. It met a similar fate: short-lived audience approval, slightly greater financial reward but critical derision, in which Chamfort detected, perhaps too readily, that ineradicable disease of the literary world: envy.

Would tragedy work better? He had been working on one for years; his name was also beginning to be mentioned in Versailles as well as Paris, and it was the new King, Louis XVI, who in 1776 commanded a performance of the play in the royal palace of Fontainebleau. It was a noble tragedy in verse, after – a very long way after – the style of Racine. But luck was on Chamfort's side: the pathetic theme was the sad fate of two fond brothers and the King, greatly

attached to his own younger brother, the Comte
d'Artois, was moved; the Queen Marie-Antoinette
openly wept (as fashion not only allowed but almost
required). Chamfort was awarded a pension on the
spot and gained the all-important royal favour which
he was never to lose. He was made reader to the Comte
d'Artois and, with his pension increased, was later to
become secretary to the King's sister Elisabeth, to
whose library he added not only *Robinson Crusoe* (cf.
No. 114) but *The Thousand and One Nights* (doubtless
suitably expurgated), as well as, prophetically,
Gibbon's *Decline and Fall of the Roman Empire* –
excellent examples of his own wide reading. It should
be noted, however, that royal pensions, however
generous, were always paid vastly in arrears: wars,
extravagant prodigality and financial incompetence
had reduced the Treasury to a ruinous shambles.

As for Chamfort's tragedy, the public of Paris had
no reason to share the new King's sentimentality and
history repeated itself: brief success at the *Comédie-
Française*, then oblivion, with the critics having a more
justifiable field day by producing evidence that
Chamfort had made borrowings from an earlier play
on the same theme. Fortunately, before the play
was put on, Chamfort had been in contact with

Beaumarchais, fresh from his triumphal *Barber of Séville*, and had joined his group of dramatists to ensure fairer deals from the notoriously stingy *Comédie-Française*. The result was that he received for his tragedy the respectable sum of 3500 *livres*[4].

Challenges to authority are infectious. It was at about this time that Chamfort became a Freemason, that constant thorn in the flesh of the Church. He had already become acquainted with another thorn in that flesh – the revolutionary bishop Talleyrand, soon to be excommunicated for his attacks on the clergy during the Revolution, who was later to co-author with Chamfort a proposal to reform France's education system. Chamfort was also establishing a close relationship with the self-styled 'plebeian' Count Mirabeau whose vigorous, inflammatory oratory, frequently based on Chamfort's ideas and expressed in Chamfort's own words, made him a leading revolutionary figure until his premature death, brought about by his excesses, particularly sexual, in 1791. Mirabeau is the M... of No. 314.

The failure of his tragedy finally forced Chamfort to face the truth that he would never achieve 'true fame' in the theatre, though, rather than admitting that he was no dramatist, he blamed public taste. Sour grapes? Certainly; but there were other more pressing reasons for him to retreat, as he now increasingly did, from the society he had expected, too confidently, to conquer. One of them he could hardly blame on anyone but himself: his health. 'Take what you want, says God, take it … and pay for it' – a Spanish proverb expressed by the more down-to-earth French as: 'Everything has to be paid for, particularly pleasure.' In the sixties and early seventies, Chamfort had been sowing acres of wild oats and his theatrical career had brought him into contact (the expression is apt) with notoriously loose-living dancers and actresses. In the early seventies, he contracted a most unpleasant disease, the exact nature of which is unknown, although malicious tongues spoke of syphilis, others, less plausibly, of leprosy and even elephantiasis. Modern medical opinion has settled, indecisively, on granulomatosis – a disagreeable word for a rather repulsive condition: the formation of scab-like tissue, externally and internally. It is both debilitating and disfiguring: adieu Hercules, adieu Adonis! There are palliative treatments, such as spa-waters – very costly for someone permanently hard-up. Friends rallied round and spas seem at least to have brought Chamfort in touch with influential circles. The disease also had frequent and prolonged intermissions, but the sword of Damocles was permanently poised: stoicism needed to replace epicureanism, and a rosy view of life became more difficult.

There were, indeed, many compensations. The King's support continued, and at the beginning of the eighties, two further comforts came his way. The first realised a hope and an ambition: in 1781, he was finally elected to the French Academy, where his good friend d'Alembert was now permanent secretary. But the honour came too late and, perversely, he proved anything but assiduous in his attendance. His 'Reflections' referring to the Academy are not flattering, and during the Revolution he was to collaborate in a report proposing its abolition.

But the second was a miracle: in 1780, this confirmed bachelor, an ailing and prematurely aged misogynist, met and fell deeply in love with the lively and attractive wife – shortly to become the widow – of the surgeon to the Comte d'Artois's bodyguard. She was more than ten years older than Chamfort and as much in love with him as he with her. They decided to fulfil the rarely realised dream of so many city-dwellers of taking refuge in the country, where they lived blissfully in communion with nature and each other. We shall never know how long this idyll might have lasted: just six months later Madame Buffon suddenly died.

At first inconsolable, Chamfort was coaxed back to Paris by young, devoted aristocratic friends. We hear of a brief, hopeless and despairing infatuation – a typically inconsistent yet understandable quest no doubt for some sort of tender consolation – but his love of women was now as dead as his love of society. It was now, towards the mid-eighties, that he turned, first, towards the expression of his acquired wisdom which, paradoxically, was to lead to posthumous fame; the only sort that he eventually considered worth enjoying, the quiet, considered esteem, not of partisan public opinion, so often influenced by envy or self-interest, but of decent, honourable people. Secondly, he turned to the pursuit of social equity, which, equally paradoxically, was to lead to his death.

In 1789 he enthusiastically supported the fall of the Bastille; his love of justice overcame his mistrust of mankind. As he wrote in Reflection No. 397, you can hardly hope to reform mankind if you assume that they are incorrigible; he still retained vestiges of his ideal-ism. Although he never became an active politician, knowing himself too well and realising that such a role would be impossible for someone in poor health and with an indestructible spirit of independence, self-respect and a strict sense of honour, he was, however, able to coin telling slogans, the most famous of which was: 'Death to the châteaux, life to the cottages!' (Later he replaced the revolutionary rallying-cry, 'Fraternity or Death!' with his own disillusioned and bitter version: 'Be my brother or I'll kill you!')

He was for a time a leading member of the most important revolutionary club of the *Jacobins* but quickly defected, like his more famous contemporary, Laclos, equally hostile to fanaticism, as soon as the club was taken over by extremists backed by the bloodthirsty Paris mob. He preferred the more moderate faction of the *Girondins* (many of whose members came from that most civilised region of France, the birthplace of Montaigne, Montesquieu – and claret. While continuing to write excellent articles recording the unfolding events of the Revolution, he also, somewhat reluctantly, accepted an appointment as chief administrator of the National Library, a post for which he was admirably suited. But the moderates did not last long. Madame Rolland, the wife of the *Girondin* leader, went to the guillotine uttering the legendary and prophetic words: 'Oh, Liberty, what crimes are committed in thy name!' And Chamfort was himself denounced (by an unscrupulous member of his staff, who wanted his job) as approving Charlotte Corday's assassination of the murderous ruffian Marat. Briefly imprisoned, on his release he resigned his post and was reduced to poverty, having lost his stipend, his free lodgings, and forced to provide, at his own expense, for the guard appointed to keep him permanently under surveillance. He heard that he was again suspect and, determined never again to accept a loss of his freedom, he tried to commit suicide, first by blowing out his brains (succeeding only in blowing out his right eye), then by stabbing himself in the chest and, in the classical manner, opening his veins. He still survived, sought refuge with friends, and seemed to be recovering when, apparently through a blunder of his doctor, he suffered a sudden relapse and died in 1794.

After his death, boxes containing thousands of scraps of paper were found in his room on which, over a considerable period, probably most actively in the mid-eighties, he had written down his thoughts on life, people and society, as well as anecdotes inspired by public or private happenings, past and present and culled from many sources: newspapers, memoirs (Duclos's access to the royal archives was very helpful), acquaintances, remarks overheard and so on (a number of them in this selection are trivial, included in order to throw light on the full spectrum). We can only surmise, from internal evidence or particular references, the dates when they were written. And we have no way of knowing in what form he might have wanted to have them published, or if, indeed, he wanted to have them published at all.

A further complication is that before their first, partial, publication a year after his death, it is known that a number of them, possibly even two thousand, had been stolen, perhaps because they were too incriminating or defamatory of people still living and too high-placed to be criticised. One document survived which mentioned a title: *Produits de la civilisation perfectionnée* (*Products of an Advanced State of Civilisation*) – an obvious, typically Chamfortian, irony. Chamfort had also suggested some subdivisions: 'Maxims', 'Thoughts', 'Characters' and 'Anecdotes'. But the distinguishing lines are very unclear; 'Maxims' and 'Thoughts' overlap and the division into 'Characters' is impossible to maintain. La Bruyère, in his *Caractères*, had mainly produced portraits of disguised, but usually recognisable, contemporary figures, but Chamfort's papers contain practically nothing of this sort.

These texts thus represent an academic nightmare – and a paradise for the anthologist, who can juggle them at will. The present solution has been to form two main divisions: the 'Reflections and Anecdotes' form one, and 'Little Philosophical Dialogues' the other; 'Reflections' and 'Anecdotes' being lumped together in the same division because of the unavoidable overlap between them. And why should they not overlap? Chamfort's character itself was full of overlaps. It is for this reason particularly that this anthology has avoided the use of the term 'maxim', too closely associated in many readers' minds with the some-what dogmatic and reductive moralist of the previous century, La Rochefoucauld, who simplistically sees all human actions as motivated, consciously or uncon-sciously, by pure self-interest.

Chamfort is far more subtle, more sensitive, more aware of his own inconsistencies, more human. Indeed, readers of this book will realise as early as Reflection No. 2 that they will be reading a sort of autobiography which, while not chronological like the *Essays* of Chamfort's favourite author Montaigne, offer considerable simi-larities, although, living in a more blatantly frivolous and openly unjust society,

Chamfort is more abrasive, and consciously (and fashionably) witty, even if less comprehensive.

The qualities of such an acute and engaging moralist have found many distinguished and enthusiastic admirers, from Stendhal, Balzac and Mérimée to Proust, Céline and Camus in France; the pessimistic Schopenhauer and Nietzsche in Germany; the great Russian poet Pushkin; in England, in more recent times, Cyril Connolly in *The Unquiet Grave* includes large passages from Chamfort; Samuel Beckett turns some of his maxims into verse; a character from Julian Barnes's novel *Love, etc* quotes from him; the contemporary author of the widely read *The Consolations of Philosophy*, Alain de Botton, is a devotee.

How can we explain this enduring appeal? Obviously the caustic wit and constantly original analogies of his robust and elegant style are attractive, but, as Einstein reminds us, 'elegance is for tailors' and Chamfort offers far more substantial and fundamental causes to continue to read him today, which are to be found in the first two Reflections. The first states a truism often ignored by the minds he describes as lazy and mediocre: circumstances alter cases and everything must be subjected to a careful and intelligent scrutiny in its context; secondly, in Reflection No. 2, he frankly states that the writer's own approach is a major concern: the honest admission of his inconsistencies involves accepting the subjectivity of his comments and admitting that truth, at best, is a personal approximation. The modernity – or even post-modernity – of this conclusion is plain: even for scientists, truth is transient, to be found in pluralism.

We are unequivocally in the presence of a man who fulfils the great American pragmatist William James's definition of philosophy: 'The peculiarly stubborn effort to think clearly'; and the reader of this selection quickly realises that, in addition to his wit, Chamfort offers the spice of endless curiosity, to include many emotions as well as all sorts of trivia, which, under his penetrating gaze, are often less trivial than at first appears; he's full of practical advice and acute insights for conducting our daily lives. His concerns are personal as well as universal, and these daily personal concerns are far from petty. It is certainly not petty to insist that dogmatism and fanaticism of any sort are to be rejected, and, paradoxically, Chamfort even condemns excess of virtue as contrary to nature (vide No. 457). And both the Reflections and the Anecdotes constantly reflect the same view: be independent, refuse to kow-tow to dictatorship by any oligarchy, be it aristocratic, plutocratic, bureaucratic (cf. his comments on royal ministers, *passim*), or proletarian; factions are all made up of individuals, who are liable to be nasty, and often of large groups of people, which makes them even nastier – and more dangerous. This warning is hardly likely to prove superfluous or outdated today, having just left a century which fanaticism turned into probably one of the bloodiest in recorded history.

Chamfort's mistrust of Man, especially in large groups, inspires his urgent call for prudence, with humbug as his main target. We can be fairly sure that modern technologies such as television, trick photography, the appropriately named computer 'web', with others doubtless still to come, will offer ample opportunity to any unscrupulous media users, e.g. in marketing, journalism, editing or even, *horresco referens*, in politics, to mislead the public; we have every reason, as Chamfort advises, to be on our guard.

Chamfort has a great deal to say about love, and it is always interesting to read the views of an expert, while making due allowance for the type of society on which his views are based, in particular his comments on marriage, conditioned by the prevailing cynicism which turned marriage into a business deal and marriage vows often into a joke in bad taste. Yet the careful reader will find that this bachelor misogynist reveals a great deal of tender understanding of those women sensitive enough to suffer as victims of this oppressive system – though he certainly knew a lot who didn't feel oppressed and, in the spirit of his age, seized the opportunities of this knowledge to enjoy them. Be that as it may, no one has made wiser and more acute observations on love than those of Nos. 223 (very pre-Proustian) and 234; some of his Reflections on love would not be disowned by any Romantic. He also comments sensitively and amusingly on children; his remarks on parenthood will sound a sympathetic chord in many a mother's heart – and put a wry smile on many a father's face.

His general moral philosophy is a basic mixture of epicureanism and stoicism, well-weighed, tried and tested; here he faced the same sort of problem as La Bruyère, who complained that he was born too late, since men had been reflecting on life for more than seven thousand years, and everything had already been said. Chamfort, like his predecessor, solved this problem by saying old things in his own witty way and simply refusing to worry if, at times, he seemed contradictory. Not surprisingly, the resulting blend, often disconcerting, is far from platitudinous, and though such a morality may seem egotistic and certainly not based on Christian charity and submission (an aspect of his thought of particular appeal to Nietzsche), it remains a valid stance for a man himself too proud to accept indiscriminate charity and fully prepared to face up to the consequences. As he amusingly points out, if we are to love our neighbour as ourselves, why shouldn't we at least love ourselves as much as our neighbour? Moreover, his attitude during the Revolution leaves us in no doubt that, however pessimistic his view of human nature, he was capable of generous, disinterested action and self-sacrifice. To quote William James again: 'There is something wild and heroic at the heart of us.'

All these are matters of high seriousness, universal problems of human existence, but if his admirers are honest (and any true admirer of Chamfort must be an enemy of cant), it's perhaps not this seriousness that mainly appeals to his readers but the witty, pithy and often impudent irreverence that he shows, not only towards the people and society of his day (especially the clergy) but also towards himself – his perceptive, caustic comments, often enlivened by vivid, unexpected imagery. We have no difficulty in recognising here our own modern world, the people around us – and ourselves. He beguilingly imposes his vision on us by reformulating the classical precept of Horace, later echoed by La Fontaine, 'to please and instruct', into the more playful, rather rococo, 'observe, suggest and entertain'. The result can be disquieting, even shocking – when certainty disappears, strange areas open up – but always thought-provoking; and Chamfort makes it comical. Isn't it possible, he suggests, that the major Consolation of Philosophy is a (sardonic) sense of humour? Agree with him or not – he's persuasive, not a bully – we'll surely not be bored; he is that very rare, most attractive, and highly addictive, bird, a pessimist who can cheer you up, a tonic guide to a modern humanism, a sceptic still believing in the possibility of decent conduct, a sense of honour, self-respect and loyalty between friends, a philosophical pluralist who never falls into outright moral relativism. He leaves us just a little room for hope – and quite a lot to smile at.

Douglas Parmée

REFLECTIONS
AND
ANECDOTES

1

Like summaries, maxims seem to have been produced
by the intelligent and accepted by mediocre or lazy
people to save themselves the trouble which has been
spent creating them; feeling excused from any further
effort, they may well give a maxim a wider meaning
than its author intended – unless the author is
mediocre himself, which can happen. A more
intelligent reader immediately realises the different
factors which make a maxim more or less applicable in
some cases or quite inapplicable in others.

Equally, in the natural sciences, the urge to
simplify creates classifications, based on the ability to
observe and compare relationships. But a scientist of
genius realises that nature contains so many individual

differences that such classifications are inadequate, whereas those with mediocre or lazy minds accept them.

There's a connection between these two sorts of mind, in fact, they're frequently identical, it's just cause and effect.

2

My whole life is an apparent contradiction of my principles: I dislike monarchy and serve a prince and a princess. I am well known for my republican principles yet I have a number of aristocratic friends plastered with royal decorations. I've chosen to be poor and enjoy it, while spending my time with the rich. I despise honours, and yet, when offered, have accepted some. Literature is almost my only consolation but I don't frequent any bright, witty people – nor do I attend sessions of the French Academy. What's more, I think that men need illusions, while having none myself. I consider that passion has more to offer than reason and I no longer feel any sort of passion. Indeed, the list is endless.

3

Most compilers of anthologies of poetry or of epigrams are like people eating cherries or oysters:

they start by picking out the best and end up eating the lot[5].

4

It would be fascinating to read a book listing all the ideas that corrupt society, morally and intellectually, but which are taken for granted or expounded in the works of the most celebrated and revered authors; ideas favouring religious superstition, unsound political principles, despotism, class snobbery, in fact every sort of popular prejudice. You'd find that almost all books contain material which corrupts – and that even the best of them do almost as much harm as good.

5

People can never stop writing about education, and such works have, in fact, produced a few interesting ideas, useful methods of teaching, in short, have provided some benefit. But what's the good of any of them without appropriate legislative or religious reforms or change in public opinion? As the aim of education is to teach the current views in these three areas, what's the point when these three aims are in conflict? What are you doing except making a child aware of the absurdity of the opinions and morality sanctioned by current religious, social and legislative authorities and teaching them to regard them with contempt?

6
Civilisation is like cooking. Seeing light, wholesome, well-prepared food on the table, you're delighted that cookery has become something of a science. However, when you see all those fancy *salsas*, complicated *coulis* and truffle *pâté* concoctions, you feel like cursing cooks and their deadly art. Doesn't the same principle apply to civilisation?

7
In the present state of society, man seems to me misled more by his reason than by his passions. His passions (I'm referring to his basic passions) have managed to preserve that small amount of natural feeling which still exists in the present social order.

8
Society isn't, as people tend to believe, a natural system: it's a decadent one, a completely new structure, cobbled together from the old system. You look at what's left with a mixture of pleasure and surprise. It's like suddenly hearing, in a social

gathering, someone expressing a simple, natural feeling. Your pleasure may even be enhanced if the person uttering it is a person of rank, that is, more remote from nature; it's charming in a king because he's at the top of the scale. It's like seeing, in a crude modern building, an antique Doric or Corinthian column.

9

A lowly peasant or a beggar can accept being looked down on without feeling demeaned, if it's merely because of his outward appearance. However, if this beggar allows his personal integrity to be questioned, even by the most exalted figure in the world, he will be as despicable in his person as in his social status.

10

It must be admitted that in society it's impossible to avoid occasionally having to play-act. The distinction between a gentleman and a rogue is that the first play-acts only when forced or to protect himself, whereas the rogue actively looks for opportunities to do so.

11

People in society often reason very oddly; if you're
standing up for someone, they'll accuse you of doing
it because he's a friend of yours. 'Yes, of course he's
my friend. But he wouldn't be my friend if he were
guilty of what you accuse him of. You're confusing
cause and effect: can't you see that he's my friend
because he's a nice man who deserves to be liked?'

12

There are two sorts of politicians and moralists:
those who see only the unpleasant or absurd side
of human nature – that's the majority – Lucian,
Montaigne, La Bruyère, La Rochefoucauld, Swift,
Mandeville, Helvétius, etc.; and those who see only
man's finer qualities, when he's reached perfection,
like Shaftesbury and a few others. The first sort know
only the latrines of a palace, the second are romantics
who carefully avoid seeing anything that might offend
them, even though it exists. The truth lies somewhere
in between.

13

If you'd like proof of the utter futility of all
preaching and moralising, think of the notion of an
hereditary nobility. Is there a single prejudice which

philosophers, orators and poets have satirised more bitterly, which has aroused greater concern, excited harsher criticism from writers of every sort? And has any of this put an end to presentations at Court or to a liking for driving around in a carriage? Has anyone stopped the practice of prying into people's pedigrees?

14

All dramatists try to produce an effect; the difference between a good and a bad one is that the first tries to do so credibly while the second kind uses any trick they can find. It's the difference between a true gentleman and a fraud — gentlemen use honest means; for the others, anything goes.

15

Philosophy's like medicine: lots of drugs, few remedies, and hardly any complete cures.

16

According to current ideas of decency, for the general public and in society, to avoid being accused of hypocrisy, the ordinary parish priest must have some sort of religious belief, though not so much as to make him intolerant; the Pope may smile if he hears

someone criticising religion, bishops can openly
laugh, while a cardinal will contribute a comment of
his own.

17

It was said of one bishop that he'd been created to
show how far the human skin can stretch.

18

I've seen men with a very ordinary, unsophisticated
ability to think, not very lofty or extensive, but
enough to enable them to expose vanity and stupidity
in their true colours, to give them a sense of
dignity and the power of recognising dignity in
others. I've seen women similarly gifted, women of
feeling, tried and proven by their experiences from
their earliest years, who'd reached the same level
of understanding. From this I deduce that people
who show great respect for such vanity and
stupidity belong to a very inferior order of
mankind.

19

Anyone who, at the right moment, can't resort to a
joke, and who lacks flexibility, very often finds he
has to cover himself by lying or being supercilious;

a predicament from which a normal man can, with propriety, easily and gracefully extricate himself with a laugh.

20

To the very young some opinions or customs seem absurd, but as you grow older you realise the reason behind them and they seem less absurd. Are we to conclude that certain customs aren't as ridiculous as they seem? There are times when you feel that they've been created by people who've read the book of life from cover to cover and that they're being judged by those who, however intelligent, have read only a few pages.

21

In some traveller's tale I read that certain African tribes believe in the immortality of the soul, though they don't claim to know what happens to it after death. They think of it as wandering about in the wilderness surrounding their village and even spend several days searching for it. Failing to find it, they go home and stop thinking about it. This is more or less what *philosophes* have done – and by far the best thing to do.

22

An honourable man enjoys the good opinion of others without thinking twice about it, almost in spite of himself. Anybody who sets out to search for it is revealing his true character.

23

There's a marvellous allegory in the Bible about the Tree of Knowledge of good and evil which causes death. Doesn't this suggest that once you've achieved a basic understanding of things and lost all your illusions, your soul dies and you become utterly impervious to all those things that so concern and worry other people?

24

It takes all sorts to make a world; even in the false complexities of our social system, men do exist who stand up for nature against society, truth against public opinion, reality against convention. This is very encouraging for your own mind and character and you can achieve a greater impact than you might expect; people do actually exist to whom you only need to reveal the truth and they'll pursue it with naïve enthusiasm; they're amazed that something so remarkable (once you've shown it in the right light) had hitherto escaped their notice.

25
In society, people pity the deaf. Isn't this just conceit? Aren't they really thinking: 'How dreadful it must be for someone not to be able to hear what I'm saying?'

26
Thinking offers consolation for everything. Even if it sometimes makes you feel sad, use it to cure your sadness and it will.

27
There's no doubt that some outstanding figures can be found in modern history – and that it's impossible to understand how they've come about. They seem out of place, like caryatids[6] set up on the wrong floor.

28
The most philosophical attitude towards society is a blend of good-humoured sarcasm and indulgent contempt.

29
I've often seen social climbers, who, in their effort to

achieve celebrity, are willing to sacrifice the good opinion of decent people and their own peace of mind.

30
One would like evil people to be lazy and stupid ones to keep their mouths shut.

31
How many distinguished soldiers, even generals, have died and are forgotten! How much less fortunate they are than Bucephalus[7] or the mastiff Berecillo, used by the Spanish to devour the indigenous inhabitants of Santo Domingo, who was paid three times as much as the common soldier!

32
The best way to explain why dishonest men, sometimes even fools, almost always have greater success in society than the honest and intelligent is that they find it easier to adapt, since, generally speaking, society is both dishonest and foolish; honest, sensible people find it difficult to come to terms with this so quickly and waste valuable time before they can hope to succeed. The former are like merchants who speak the language of the country and

can start trading straight away, whereas the latter are forced to learn the speech of their suppliers and clients. Before setting up shop and starting business, they often can't even be bothered and leave without making a single deal.

33

A soldier in an army composed of Catholics, Lutherans and Calvinists was fatally wounded and couldn't remember what he believed in himself, so he asked a fellow comrade what the best religion was, to which the soldier who wasn't interested in such matters replied that he'd no idea and advised him to ask their captain. When consulted, the captain replied that he'd pay a great deal to know the answer himself.

34

Foolishness can seem very smart and there are some very smartly dressed fools.

35

In order to forgive reason for the harm it causes so many people, you mustn't forget what these people's situation would be without it. Reason is a necessary evil.

36

Sometimes our reason makes us as unhappy as our passions; in such cases, you could say that you're a sick man poisoned by your doctor.

37

If, the day after Cain killed Abel, Adam had been told that a few centuries later in Paris some seven or eight hundred thousand people would be piled up all together in one single enclosed space of some twelve square miles, would he have been able to conceive that such a multitude could possibly live side by side? Wouldn't he have had an even more terrifying idea of the monstrous crimes likely to be committed? We must always keep this in mind to console ourselves for the abuses arising from such extraordinary conglomerations of human beings.

38

What's a philosopher? He's someone who sets nature against law, reason against custom, his own private convictions against public opinion and his own judgement against error.

39

The prudence of an eagle is superior to the prudence

of a mole; it means boldly following the dictates of your character and bravely accepting all the setbacks and hardships which may result.

40

The physical world seems to be the work of a good and powerful being, forced to leave part of his programme to be completed by some evil creature; but the moral world seems to have been created by some capricious, demented Devil.

41

Never set yourself aims beyond your reach, either privately or publicly.

42

Courtiers are poor men who've got rich by begging.

43

Most society people are so thoughtless and scatterbrained that they have no real idea of the world around them. 'And the reason for that,' a gentleman of my acquaintance used to say, 'is the same that makes may bugs ignorant of natural history.'

44

In society there are very few things which any decent man can feel comfortable with, in his heart or his mind.

45

In important matters, men display themselves as they want to be seen; in minor matters as they really are.

46

A stupid man showing a brief glimmer of intelligence creates the same feeling of surprise and shock as a cab-horse breaking into a gallop.

47

Instead of trying to correct the intolerable way some people behave, we'd do better to correct the weakness of character of the people who let them get away with it.

48

Most acts of folly are the result of sheer stupidity.

49

Public opinion reigns in society because stupidity reigns amongst the stupid.

50

We must be allowed to behave as stupidly as our
character requires.

51

Few people are prepared to use their reason without
fear or favour, or bold enough to apply it relentlessly
to every moral, political and social issue: to kings and
ministers, to men in high places, to the *philosophes*,
to absolutely every scientific and artistic principle,
etc. And if we don't, we're doomed to remain
mediocre.

52

There are people who feel the need to be prominent,
to rise above their fellow men, at all costs. Their
whole concern is to play the charlatan in full view
of everyone: on the stage, on the throne or on the
gallows, they'll always feel fine as long as they're
the centre of attention.

53

Herding together diminishes people. It's like Milton's
devils, forced to turn into pygmies to get into
Pandemonium[8].

54

The power of reason is one of nature's most important gifts; it enables you to rise above your passions and weaknesses and even to control your better qualities – your talents and virtues.

55

For fear of attracting attention, we're ready to suppress our real personality, and in order to escape notice, we'll take refuge in oblivion.

56

Physical calamities and natural disasters forced us to live in communities. Living in communities added to these natural problems; the drawbacks of living in society led to our need to be governed and government increases social evils. You've just read a resumé of the history of mankind.

57

Petty souls are more susceptible to ambition than great ones, just as straw or thatched cottages burn more easily than palaces.

58

The fable of Tantalus has generally been regarded

as symbolising avarice. It's at least equally applicable to ambition, love of fame, indeed to almost every passion.

59

All passions involve excess, in fact that's what makes them passions.

60

The philosopher who attempts to extinguish his passions is like a chemist trying to put out a fire he's lit himself.

61

A man who prefers his own company needs to be a good man; if he prefers the company of other people, he needs to be honourable.

62

Nature has decreed that wise men and fools both have illusions; this is to prevent the wise man from becoming too unhappy as a result of his wisdom.

63

By endowing us at birth with reason and passion,

nature seems to be trying to mitigate the dire effects
of the former by the use of the latter; by allotting
us only a few more years to live once we've been
deprived of passion, she seems to be taking pity on
us by freeing us from an existence in which we'd
be left with reason as our only resource.

64

Seeing how people are treated in hospitals, you
might imagine that these institutions are not
intended to cure the sick but to keep them out of
sight of those lucky members of society whose
pleasures would be spoiled if they saw these poor
wretches.

65

These days, anyone who loves nature is accused
of living in a world of pure fantasy.

66

Tragedies suffer from the moral defect of attaching
too great an importance to life and death.

67

The most misspent day in any life is the one when
you've failed to laugh.

68

Your intelligence often bears the same relation to your heart as the library of a château does to its owner.

69

Poets, orators, even *philosophes*, say the same things about fame that we were told as boys to encourage us to win prizes. What they tell children to make them prefer being praised by their nannies to eating jam tarts is the same idea constantly drummed into us to encourage us to sacrifice our real interests in the hope of being praised by our contemporaries or by posterity.

70

If you want to become a philosopher you mustn't allow yourself to be put off by your first unpleasant discoveries about the human race. To learn about mankind, you have to ignore the disappointments they cause you, just as the anatomist needs to overcome his initial disgust and ignore his own organs in order to learn the necessary skills to practise his art.

71

By coming to terms with nature's ills, you learn to

despise death; by coming to terms with the ills of society, you come to despise life.

72
A man's worth is like that of a diamond, where a certain degree of perfection, purity and size have a recognised fixed value, beyond which they become priceless and will never find a buyer.

73
The public refuses to believe that certain qualities and feelings can be sincere and, generally speaking, finds it impossible to understand anything but the lowest ideas.

74
There are times when public opinion is the worst possible opinion.

75
There are those who, not particularly pleasant in themselves, don't stop other people from being so. Their company is sometimes perfectly tolerable. There are others who are not only unpleasant in themselves, but whose very presence inhibits others from showing how agreeable they are capable of

being. Such people are intolerable: this is the great disadvantage of pedantry.

76

There's no man who, singly, is as contemptible as a body of men. There's no single body of men that can be as contemptible as the general public.

77

Hope is a fake which constantly misleads us; I only achieved happiness myself once I'd given up hoping. Over the entrance to my Paradise, I'd gladly write what Dante put over the entrance to his Inferno: '*All hope abandon, ye who enter here.*'

78

A poor man not dependent on anybody is controlled only by necessity; a rich man dependent on others is controlled by someone else or by a number of people.

79

What do you gain by having fewer weaknesses than other people? Does it give them less hold over you? One weakness is enough, once it's become common knowledge. You need to be Achilles without his heel and, unfortunately, that seems to be an impossibility.

80

See what happens when a completely absurd and unjust claim involving other people's interests, a claim which would be dismissed with contempt by any group of decent men, comes before a legal tribunal. The result is a pure lottery: any lawsuit is equally likely to be won or lost. Similarly, if any statement, any opinion, however ridiculous, comes up for discussion by the different factions of any assembly, any body of men, you may well find a majority of voters supporting it.

81

It's a well-recognised fact that our age has redefined the meaning of certain words and by eliminating any purely intellectual or highfaluting niceties, has made moral, political and practical issues simpler and more straightforward.

To take just one example, the question of what is moral: we can see how many complex metaphysical factors are involved in the concept of honour. Our age has realised how inconvenient this is and to reduce the matter to its simplest terms and avoid any misunderstanding has decided that the word may be applied to anyone who hasn't actually been found guilty of a criminal offence.

In earlier days, the word gave rise to all sorts of ambiguities and misconceptions; now nothing could be more straightforward: has a man ever suffered a conviction? That's all we need to know. It's purely a matter of fact, which can be checked by consulting the relevant police records. If a man hasn't ever been convicted, then he's a man of honour and can claim to be admitted anywhere, such as to government office, etc. He can become a member of any corporate body, any academy, the highest courts of justice.

You can understand how such precision, such accuracy removes any possibility of dispute or quibbling and how human relations become far easier – and so much more convenient.

82

Fame often exposes an honourable man to the same tribulations as wealth, that is to say that in order to achieve either, both are forced to do or to accept things which go against the grain. Anyone determined to remain entirely honourable has to reject either fame or wealth, and either face obscurity or hardship – perhaps even both.

83

Anybody placed at exactly the same distance between yourself and your enemy will always appear to be closer to your enemy. It's an optical illusion, just as the jet of a fountain seems closer to the other side than to yours.

84

Public opinion is a jurisdiction that no honourable man will ever completely accept but never completely reject.

85

So desire for fame is to be admired? How odd to admire something which relies on all sorts of vice, is spurred on by pride, ambition, every kind of vanity, and sometimes even by greed.

86

It's generally held that the best way to achieve success is to be agreeable. But an infinite capacity to be bored gives far better results; making money as well as success with women can be reduced almost entirely to this gift.

87

There are few men of character who haven't some romantic element in their nature. A man entirely lacking it, however decent or intelligent, will, in comparison with a really great man, be like a highly skilled artist who feels no aspiration towards an ideal beauty, compared to a genius who is the living embodiment of this idea.

88

There are men whose genius shines more brightly in private than in public life, where he appears out of place. The lovelier a diamond is, the simpler its setting should be; if it's too showy it reduces the beauty of the diamond.

89

If you don't want to become a phoney, stay away from the stage because once you're there you'll be forced to become one, unless you want to be pelted by the audience.

90

Few vices are more certain to prevent you from having lots of friends than possessing too many virtues.

91

Life is a disease temporarily relieved every sixteen hours, by sleep. The complete cure: death.

92

Studying morals would be much easier if we could distinguish between pride and vanity. The former is noble, calm, upright, quiet, unshakeable; the latter base, fickle, restless, uneasy, vacillating. One is the source of a great many virtues, the other of every kind of vice and weakness. There's a sort of pride which follows every one of God's commandments and certain types of vanity that include the seven deadly sins.

93

There's a certain type of pretentiousness which can be quashed by simply paying no attention to it; and there's another sort that is reduced to impotence when you don't even notice it.

94

Nature seems to use men for her own ends, with no concern for the instruments she's using, rather like tyrants who discard someone once he's served their purpose.

95

In order not to find life unbearable, you must accept two things: the ravages of time and the injustices of man.

96

For me, wisdom includes distrust. The Bible says the beginning of wisdom is fear of God. I think it starts with fear of man.

97

The great disadvantage of passion is not so much the suffering it causes you as the evil, degrading actions it makes you commit. Otherwise, it'd be far more attractive than cold reason which can never bring happiness.

Passion makes you live, reason merely helps you survive.

98

Petty people can never be truly kind; at best they can show kindliness.

99

We ought to be able to combine opposites: love of goodness with indifference to other people's opinions,

a liking for work with indifference to fame, concern
for our health with indifference to life.

100
A man without principles is usually a man lacking
character, otherwise he'd have felt the need to provide
himself with some.

101
Sometimes when an evil person does something good,
it's as if they are trying to discover if doing good
gives as much pleasure as good people claim.

102
Between an intelligent evil person and an intelligent
honourable one there's the same difference as between
a clever murderer and a man of honour who's an
excellent swordsman.

103
An ambitious man who's in despair when he's failed to
reach his goal reminds me of Ixion who was sent to
hell for trying to embrace a cloud.

104
If the cruel truths, the unpleasant discoveries, the

hidden secrets of society, which any man of the world will have become aware of by the age of forty, had been known to him twenty years before, he would either have been plunged into despair or else become corrupt; yet we do meet a small number of wise men of forty who, despite knowing all these things, are neither corrupt nor unhappy. Their prudence and goodness have guided them through this maze of corruption, and their strength of character and breadth of understanding have enabled them to overcome the sadness inspired by the perversity of the human race.

105

You can safely bet that any generally accepted idea or conventional belief is foolish since it's been approved by the majority.

106

Being respected is better than being celebrated, enjoying people's good opinion is better than being eminent, and being honourable is better than being famous.

107

To help a man suffering from dropsy, it's far better

to cure his thirst than to offer him a barrel of wine.
Apply this principle to the wealthy.

108
Weak people are the light infantry of the army of the
wicked. They cause more harm than the army itself;
they spread infection, they wreak havoc.

109
It's often easier to make something legal than to make
it legitimate.

110
You have to agree that, in order to live at ease in high
society, there are certain sides to your character that
you have to completely paralyse.

111
Celebrity: the advantage of being known by people
who don't know you.

112
It's not true, as Rousseau claimed, following Seneca,
that the more you think, the less you feel; but it is
true that the more you judge, the less you love. Few
people tempt you to make any exception to this rule.

113

There's a sort of pleasure in having the courage to disparage the wealthy. Despising money is like toppling a king off his throne; there's a special relish to it.

114

Having lost everything, and forced to carry out the most arduous tasks to meet his daily needs, Robinson Crusoe succeeds in living on his island and even, as he himself admits, enjoys moments of happiness. Suppose he'd been wrecked on a magic island, with everything provided to make life easy and nothing to do: mightn't he have been bored to death?

115

Men's ideas are like card-playing or any other game. Ideas which in the past I've seen considered reckless have since become commonplace, almost trivial, and adopted by men unworthy of sharing them. Ideas which now seem extraordinary will be regarded as feeble and perfectly ordinary by our descendants.

116

If you want to discover how men are corrupted by
their social status, take a look at what they're like in
their old age, after long exposure to its influence.
Look at old courtiers, judges, lawyers and surgeons,
for instance.

117

Men whose only concern is other people's opinion of
them are like actors who put on a poor performance
to win the applause of people of poor taste; some of
them would be capable of good acting in front of a
good audience. A decent man plays his part to the
best of his ability, regardless of the taste of the
gallery.

118

A cordial relationship between brothers is so unusual
that in mythology only Castor and Pollux appear as
an example of friendly brothers; and they are shown
as never meeting, as they move alternately from earth
to the Elysian Fields, thereby removing any risk of
conflict.

119

In the course of my reading, I've come to realise that

the first reaction of anyone who'd done something heroic, helped people in trouble at great personal risk or performed some outstanding public or private service, is to refuse any reward. This immediate reaction is found amongst the lowest, poorest classes. What is this moral instinct which prompts people to find their reward purely in the hearts of those they've helped? It seems as if being paid for these good deeds takes them away from us.

120

There are more men who are fools than wise, and even in the wise there's more foolishness than wisdom.

121

We're happy or unhappy for a host of unseen reasons which are never mentioned and never can be mentioned.

122

Skill is to cunning what dexterity is to picking pockets.

123

Pleasures may be based on illusion; happiness must be

based on truth, for truth alone offers whatever happiness mankind is capable of enjoying. People basing their happiness on illusion are speculators; happiness based on truth is wealth held in property and sound business.

124
Stubbornness equals character roughly as lust equals love.

125
Love is delightful and foolhardy, ambition dour and obtuse.

126
Before being generous, you must be fair; before adding ruffs to shirt sleeves, you must first have a shirt.

127
Wealth often turns out to be like those rich and extravagant wives who ruin the families to which they've brought substantial dowries.

128
The Dutch have no sympathy for debtors: they think

that anyone who runs up debts, if he's poor, is defrauding his fellow citizens, and, if rich, his heirs.

129
Weak characters think money all-important; for any well-bred person, it's a very minor concern.
However, there's still a very big difference between the man who despises money and a truly honourable man.

130
Changes in fashion are the tax levied by the poor on the rich.

131
When I hear people claiming that it's the least sensitive man who is, on the whole, the happiest, I think of the Indian saying: It's better to be sitting than standing, lying than sitting, and, best of all, to be dead rather than alive.

132
The richest person is the one who's frugal; the poorest, the miser.

133

Sometimes there are misleading similarities between the characters of two men which bring and hold them together for a while; this misunderstanding slowly evaporates; they're amazed to discover how different they really are and even repelled by each other in every respect.

134

Isn't it odd that the fame of a number of thinkers rests on having spent their lives refuting stupid prejudices which, on the face of it, ought never even to have entered anyone's head? Bayle, for example, is famous for having shown the absurdity of certain scholastic philosophical subtleties which would have made any sensible peasant shrug his shoulders; Locke's reputation is based on having proved that you mustn't talk without understanding what you're saying and shouldn't think you understand something when you don't. A number of distinguished philosophers have written learned books attacking superstitious beliefs which would make a Red Indian in Canada take flight in contempt. Montesquieu's fame and that of some of his predecessors is that, while still respecting many miserable prejudices, he did suggest that the task of those who govern is to care for the welfare of the people they're governing and not the other way round. If the dream of the *philosophes* that society is perfectible can be realised, what will posterity say when it sees that so much effort was required to reach such simple natural conclusions?

135

Anyone who relies too heavily on reason to achieve happiness, who analyses it, who, so to speak, quibbles over his enjoyment and can accept only refined pleasures, ends up not having any at all. He's like a man who wants to get rid of all the lumps in his mattress and eventually ends up sleeping on bare boards because he's made it too small.

136

A man of foresight is a rather sad figure. He disturbs his friends by predicting the problems likely to arise as a result of their imprudence, they refuse to believe him and, when he's proved right, they're amazed by the accuracy of his gloomy predictions. They feel offended, their pride is hurt, and when they meet this friend, who would have been able to console them and whom they would have approached if they hadn't felt ashamed, they feel humiliated.

137

Time reduces the intensity of what metaphysicians call absolute pleasures but it seems to enhance relative ones. I suspect this is one of nature's sly tricks to make us want to go on living after we've lost the pleasures or objects which made life worth living.

138

When you've endured a great deal of suffering and feel completely unable to bear any more, you realise that you must live from day to day, forget many things and, in a word, *erase* your life as it ebbs away.

139

They say that every day you must make an effort to reduce your needs. This principle applies specially to our conceit, whose demands are the most insistent and so need to be most strongly resisted.

140

It's not uncommon to see weak characters trying to overcome their weakness by seeking the company of people more determined and stronger-minded. This can produce the oddest results, as comical as when you see a fool trying to be intelligent.

141

Being virtuous isn't the highest form of good, no more than being healthy; it's not good in its own right but it is where good is to be found. Vice is more likely to lead to unhappiness than virtue to happiness and the best reason for being virtuous is because it's the complete opposite of being vicious.

142

As Montaigne has already pointed out, you don't learn about living from books, though he didn't say why: it's because you learn about life through hundreds of tiny observations which in our conceit we never dare to admit, even to our closest friends. We're afraid of revealing the extent to which we're preoccupied by any number of petty matters, even though these are crucial to achieving success in issues of the highest importance.

143

What sort of society is it which is not bound by reason, where there's no room for feeling, no congenial exchange of ideas, no true benevolence? It's nothing but a fair, a market-place, a gambling den, a bawdy house and *little houses*[9], that's all.

144

Once you're too old to feel passion, living in society becomes unbearable. It's tolerable only as long as you have your stomach for your enjoyment and yourself – to kill time.

145

Society can be divided into two main categories: people who have more appetite than dinners and those who have more dinners than appetite.

146

'He's a fool, a sheer fool!' – easy enough to say, but what does it really mean? He thinks he fully deserves to hold the office he does, his importance is justified, his reputation is well-earned. Doesn't everyone feel that about himself? Why make such a fuss about it?

147

The theoretical structure of society may be compared to an actual building consisting of little niches or compartments of various sizes, each representing particular jobs with their own rights, privileges, etc. The jobs are permanent, their holders come and go; sometimes they're big, at other times, small; and none, or almost none, of them fits properly into his place. In one there's a giant forced to squat down or bend double; in another there's a dwarf who's got the free run of a whole arcade. Circling round the building is a whole swarm of people of various sizes, all waiting for a vacant niche to move into, whatever the size. Each of them is proclaiming his right – meaning his birth or his patronage – to be given the post. If any of the competitors were to raise the question of matching the post and the applicant, the instrument to its case, they'd be shouted down; even the candidates themselves aren't prepared to raise any objections to their rivals on the grounds that they're likely to prove unsuitable.

148

Anything said in a club, a salon, at a dinner-party, a public meeting, is untrue or inadequate. What is true and worth hearing are the things which a decent, honest, sensible man, speaking from the heart, who's seen a lot of life and seen it clearly, tells a friend as they sit chatting round the fire. I've learned more from such conversations than from mixing in society or from reading any of my books.

149

There's one golden rule for those who enjoy teasing

and poking fun at people: make quite sure you do it properly. If the person concerned takes offence, you've done it badly.

150

We often become aware of the gap between our impressions and reality but never more strikingly than when it happens without warning. One evening, walking down a boulevard, you notice a charming garden at the end of which you can see into a dining-room, tastefully lit, and glimpse a group of pretty women, an arbour, an avenue opening up in the distance; you can hear laughter: their figures are so slim, surely they must be nymphs? You ask a passer-by who they are and he tells you the name of the mistress of the house. Unfortunately, you happen to know her: the charm vanishes in a flash.

151

M... used to warn me that I had one grave disability: I couldn't suffer fools – and their predominance – gladly. He was right and I realised that in society a fool had one great advantage: he was among his peers.

152

There are times when, seeing the nasty tricks people get up to, the gross frauds of high officials, you're tempted to think that you're in a wood infested by thieves, amongst whom the most dangerous are the police, whose purpose is supposed to be that of arresting them.

153

There are moments when society people seem ready to be assessed at their true value. I've often noticed that they appreciate those who show little regard for them, which seems a sort of invitation to express your contempt openly, providing you do it sincerely, without affectation or arrogance, and from the heart.

154

People who take a sudden liking to royalty immediately after receiving some royal honour remind me of children who want to become priests the day after seeing some impressive religious procession or want to join the army after attending a grand military parade.

155

You imagine ministers and other high officials have

principles because you've heard them say so. As a result, you avoid asking them to do anything that might cause them to break those principles. However, you soon discover you've been hoodwinked when you see ministers doing things which prove that they're quite unprincipled: it's nothing but a habit they've got into, an automatic reflex.

156
I'd advise anyone approaching a minister for a favour to look miserable rather than cheerful: nobody likes to see anyone looking happier than himself.

157
You can't imagine how clever you have to be in order never to be ridiculous.

158
The best way to put the shortcomings of society, and, indeed, of the whole of mankind, in their proper place is to joke about them. Joking allows you to avoid compromising yourself, it's a proof of your superiority over them and the things you're poking fun at, without causing offence to anyone except people who are surly or uncouth. The reputation of having such a weapon earns from society – even the

highest society – the same sort of respect for someone inferior that the military show towards a brilliant swordsman. I once heard a wit say: 'Take away the power of ridicule and you'll never see me in society again.' It's a sort of duel without bloodshed and, like the real thing, it makes men more polite and more circumspect.

159

All corporate bodies – judges, academics, assemblies – however corrupt, are buoyed up by their sheer bulk and there's nothing you can do about it. Disgrace, ridicule, everything bounces off them like bullets off the hide of a wild boar or a crocodile.

160

When you see the care social conventions seem to take to exclude anyone of true quality from every position where they could have been of service to the community and study how fools close ranks against people of intelligence, you'd think you're seeing lackeys conspiring to keep out their masters.

161

In France and elsewhere, the most absurd customs and protocol are justified by the statement: 'It's always been done like that.' That's exactly what Hottentots tell Europeans when asked why they feed on locusts or the vermin on their bodies: 'It's what we've always done.'

162

It's easy to express, in simple terms, the exact value of being well-known: anyone outstandingly talented or virtuous exposes himself to the passive goodwill of a few decent people and faces the active ill-will of every scoundrel. Calculate the size of these two groups and their relative importance.

163

Few people are able to appreciate a philosopher; he's almost a sort of public enemy. Faced by the various pretensions of mankind and the ambiguous nature of facts, he says bluntly: 'I'm prepared to take you only at your true value, what you're really worth.' And it's not easy to get people to appreciate anyone who makes such an uncompromising declaration.

164

These days a painter will dash off your portrait in seven minutes; another one will teach you how to paint in three days; someone else will tell you how to learn English in forty lessons. They'll try to get you to master eight languages by using pictures of objects with the names underneath in all eight of them. And in the end, if they could, they'd collect up all the pleasures, emotions and thoughts of a lifetime, cram them into the space of twenty-four hours, stuff this pill into your mouth and say: 'That's the lot, goodbye, off you go!'

165

If you want to make a good impression in society, you have to submit to being told all sorts of things you already know by people who don't even know them themselves.

166

You don't really know people you only half-know, and when you know three-quarters of something you don't know it at all. With these two observations in mind, you can accurately assess every discussion you'll have to listen to in society.

167

In a country where everyone's keen to show off, many people must, and indeed do, prefer to be a bankrupt rather than a nobody.

168

The threat of neglecting a cold is for doctors what purgatory is for priests: a goldmine.

169

In conversation with some millionaires, a man of intelligence was claiming that you can live quite well on six thousand *livres* a year. They sharply and indeed indignantly denied his claim. After leaving them, he tried to puzzle out the reason for the attitude of these men, who were friends of his, and finally decided that it was because, by speaking his mind, he'd shown them that he wasn't dependent on them. Anyone whose needs are small seems threatening to the rich, because he's always ready to escape their control. This is how tyrants recognise that they're losing a slave. You can apply this observation to the passions in general: a man who has overcome his passion for women is capable of showing his indifference to them, something which they always find so detestable that they immediately cease to show the slightest interest in him. Perhaps this is why nobody shows any concern for the welfare of a philosopher: as he doesn't share the passions of people in society, they realise that there's nothing much they can do to make him happy and leave him to go his own way.

170

A philosopher looks on what is known as 'social status' in the same way as Tartars look on towns; that is to say, as a prison, a circle into which people are packed and crammed together, preventing any possibility of developing or broadening your mind or spirit. A man of higher social rank has a larger, better furnished prison; anyone of inferior status lives in a dungeon. The only free man is the one who has no status at all – provided he's comfortably off or at least has no need of anyone's support.

171

Many men are prevented from becoming misanthropic either through weakness of character or through lack of ideas, in a word, by the very things that make us unable to live by ourselves.

172

Do you feel happier living by yourself than you do living in society? Could that be because, left to yourself, you can think about facts whereas in society you have to think about people.

173

Any intelligent man who lacks character is lost.

You've got to have Diogenes' stick as well as his lantern.

174
Nature didn't tell me: 'Don't be poor!'; and certainly didn't say: 'Get rich!'; but she did shout: 'Always be independent!'

175
People become servile for the same reason that the Spartans called the Persians slaves: they didn't know how to say 'No'. The ability to utter that word and to keep your own company is the only way to stay free and true to yourself.

176
Anyone who stubbornly refuses to allow the absurd and hypocritical conventions of society to force him to compromise his reason, his integrity or at least his scruples, who'll never make concessions when it's in his interest to do so, will inevitably end up isolated, since his only support will come from Virtue, that pure abstraction who'll let you starve.

177
In high society, no one has more enemies than a

proud, sensitive, upright man who prefers to leave men alone to be what they are rather than accept them for what they're not.

178

Once you've made up your mind to frequent only men capable of acting honestly, ethically, reasonably and truthfully towards you, men who view convention, vanity and etiquette as merely means to bolster up society, then this decision (which will be forced on you unless you're stupid, weak and contemptible) will be likely to result in your having to live more or less on your own.

179

Anyone lacking character isn't a man but an object.

180

Philosophers recognise four main virtues from which all the others derive: justice, moderation, strength and prudence. We can say that the first two are contained in the last one, which, in a way replaces the third, by saving the man who has the misfortune of not possessing it from most occasions when it's needed.

181

Our feelings towards most benefactors are like the gratitude we feel for our dentist. We say to ourselves that he's done a good job, and saved us from further pain, but we still can't forget how much he hurt us. We don't feel too kindly towards him.

182

Slander is like a wasp which is pestering you but which you mustn't take any action against unless you're certain of killing it, otherwise it'll come back more ferociously than ever.

183

Some men need illusions about certain matters in their lives in order to go on living. At times, however, they seem to have a vague inkling which makes you think that they're not too far from realising the truth – but which they hurriedly abandon. They're like children chasing a masked man and then taking to their heels if he happens to turn round.

184

After a certain age, any new friends we make in our attempt to replace the ones we've lost are like glass eyes, false teeth and wooden legs compared to real eyes, our own teeth and legs of flesh and bone.

185
The naïve comments of a well brought up child sometimes express a very attractive philosophy.

186
Most friendships are bristling with ifs and buts; they end up being mere acquaintances, relying on nothing more than hidden assumptions.

187
People are evil by nature and have become worse by forming into social groups. Everybody contributes, firstly, the faults inherent in mankind, secondly, one's own particular faults, and, thirdly, those faults peculiar to one's class. These faults accumulate with time and as they grow older everybody suffers from everyone else's shortcomings as well as their own and comes to regard mankind with a contempt which can only result in turning them against both.

188
Happiness is like watches: the simpler the better. A watch which strikes twice is more likely to give trouble; a minute hand makes it even more liable to

go wrong, while the one which indicates the days of the week and the month is always the first to need repair.

189

With mankind, all is vanity, their pleasures as well as their pains. But it's still better for this empty soap bubble to be blue or gold than dull grey or black.

190

Anyone disguising his tyranny, patronage or even his kindness under the mask or name of friendship reminds me of that evil priest who put poison in his sacramental wafers.

191

Stoics are an inspired sect: their moral philosophy reads like exalted romantic poetry.

192

Poverty is an invitation to crime.

193

When you see or feel the anguish caused by extreme love or friendship, either through the death of a loved one or the accidents of life, you're tempted to think that amusement and frivolity aren't so foolish after all and that life shouldn't really be taken any more seriously than it is by the pleasure-loving man about town.

194
There aren't many benefactors who don't say, like Satan to Jesus: 'All these things will I give you if you bow down and worship me.'[10]

195
In some passionate friendships, you have a double pleasure: the delights of passion endorsed by reason.

196
Take your pleasure, give pleasure to others without doing harm to yourself or to anyone else: that sums up the whole of morality.

197
For a decent, honourable man who has certain principles, God's commandments have been summarised by Rabelais over the entrance to his Abbey of Thélème: 'Do what you like.'

198

I study only the things I like; I apply my mind only to matters that interest me. They'll be useful – or useless – to me or to others and in due course, I'll be given – or not given – the opportunity of benefiting from what I've learned. In any case, I'll have enjoyed the inestimable advantage of doing things I like doing and following my own inclinations.

199

I've destroyed my passions, rather like a violent man who, finding he can't control his horse, kills it.

200

For me to accept success, it will have to meet all the conditions set by my character.

201

By turning my back on society and a successful career, I've become happy, at peace, healthy, and even rich. Ignoring the proverb: 'If at first you don't succeed...', I've thrown in my hand – and I've won.

202

One of mankind's greatest misfortunes is that sometimes even our good qualities are of no use and that the art of using and controlling them properly comes only as a result of experience – and too late.

203
I've forgotten everything I was ever taught. What little I still know came through intuition.

204
Anxiety and indecision are for the mind and the spirit what torture is for the body.

205
Education must be based on two things: ethics and prudence; ethics in order to develop your good qualities, prudence to protect you from other people's bad ones. If you attach too great an importance to goodness, you produce credulous fools; if you're too prudent, you produce self-serving, scheming rogues. The principle underlying every society is justice, for yourself and for others. If you are to love your neighbour as yourself, it's only fair to love yourself as much as you love your neighbour.

206
The perfect man is an honest man who's lost all his illusions. If he's got a mind, he's excellent company;

since he attaches no importance to anything, he can't
be a pedant; he's forbearing because he remembers
that, like those still suffering from illusions, he once
had them too. Being carefree, he's decisive in his
dealings; he never quibbles or insists. If other people
do it to him, he ignores them or brushes them aside.
He's bound to be more cheerful than anyone else
because he can always find the appropriate epigram to
apply to his fellow men. He's on the right track and
can afford to laugh at those who aren't. He's in a
well-lit area watching the foolish antics of people
stumbling around in the dark. He can demolish with a
laugh the false standards and judgements which others
apply to people and things.

207
The contemplative life is often miserable. Be more
active, stop thinking so much, don't just watch
yourself living.

208
A man may aspire to achieve virtue, but he can't
reasonably expect to discover truth.

209
Love is a feeling that in order to appear honourable

must contain no other feeling; it must exist and continue to exist exclusively for itself.

210
Remove conceit from love and there's not much left. Purged of vanity, it's a feeble convalescent, barely able to drag itself along.

211
Love is like an epidemic disease: the more scared you are of it, the more likely you are to catch it.

212
Where feelings are concerned, if you find it possible to calculate them, they're not true feelings.

213
Whenever a man and a woman feel a violent passion for each other, it seems to me that whatever the obstacles — a husband, parents, relatives, anything you like — those two people are bound to each other by a *law of nature*. They belong to each other by *divine right*, regardless of any other law or convention.

214
In modern society love has been reduced to this: two

people take a fancy to each other, two skins make contact.

215
A man in love is trying to be more lovable than he really is; that's why almost all men in love are ridiculous.

216
To persuade you to meet a woman, someone will tell you: 'She's so adorable, you'll love her!' But supposing I don't want to love her? It would be much better to say: 'She's very loving,' because more men want to be loved than to love.

217
It's amusing that, in many ancient civilisations, the expression 'knowing a woman' means going to bed with her. It's as if you can't really get to know a woman without sleeping with her.

Ancient civilisations must have been more advanced than we think.

218
A very wealthy man was talking about the poor: 'They're completely hopeless; you never give them a

thing, yet the buggers still keep coming back for more!'

219

People find it quite easy to agree that feeling makes you think; what they find more difficult is the idea that thinking can make you feel, which is almost equally true.

220

It may be that it is only possible to know real friendship if you have been in love.

221

In general, people only seem to approve of marriages based on reason, yet the only interesting marriages are the unreasonable ones. In any other form, they're nothing but a miserable calculation.

222

Marriage as practised in high society is nothing more than a socially accepted indecency.

223

It's commonly said that a woman can only give you what she's got. That's utter nonsense: she's giving you what you think you're getting, because in these matters it's your imagination which assesses the amount.

224
When you're with a woman, if you retained the slightest recollection of something you know by heart, you'd be very unhappy.

225
Society is very demeaning for men, but it reduces a woman to nothing.

226
'Any man who hasn't known lots of tarts doesn't know anything about women,' a man told me sententiously. He had no idea that his wife, whom he adored, was deceiving him.

227
In a love affair, all we need is to share each other's pleasures and attractions. But in a happy marriage, you need to love one another or at the very least be willing to share each other's shortcomings.

228

Love is pleasanter than marriage; isn't fiction more interesting than history?

229

Love captivates us by flattering our conceit: how can we possibly resist a feeling which enhances us in our own eyes, gives us back something we've lost, and adds something we haven't got?

230

Dealings between men and women resemble those practised by Europeans in India: they're warlike.

231

We've seen highly respectable men, with a reputation for decency, congratulating a beautiful and virtuous young woman on her good fortune in marrying an unhealthy, dishonest, stupid, revoltingly ugly man who is very rich. Considering such an event as a triumph and the absurdity of applauding something which flies in the face of every principle of nature and of morality typify the utter decadence of our age.

232

Being loved isn't enough, we want to be appreciated,

and that's possible only with someone similar to
ourselves. That's why love can't exist, or at least can't
last, when one of the partners is too inferior to the
other. This isn't a question of vanity but of self-
respect, which it would be absurd and impossible to
try to eliminate from human nature. Vanity is for the
weak and corrupt; decent self-respect forms part of
the natural order of things.

233

Nature has entrusted the survival of every species
to a mother's love, and, in order to ensure that she
receives her due rewards, has made them part
and parcel of the pleasures and even of the trials
and tribulations inherent in this delightful feeling.

234

In love, everything is both true and false; it's the one
subject on which it's impossible to say anything
absurd.

235

A man in love who feels sorry for a sensible man
seems to me to be like a man fond of fairy stories
poking fun at someone who prefers history.

236

However low a man's opinion of women may be, there's no woman whose opinion of them isn't even lower.

237

It would seem that by implanting in men an indestructible liking for women, nature has guessed that without this precaution the contempt inspired by the vices of the fair sex – notably their vanity – would make the propagation and survival of the human species very precarious.

238

It has been remarked that physicists, zoologists, chemists and physiologists are usually of a quiet, good-tempered and generally happy disposition whereas writers on politics or on legal matters, and even moral philosophers, are often sad and melancholy. The reason couldn't be simpler: the former are studying nature, the latter, society; the first are examining the work of the Supreme Being, the second the works of man. Is it any wonder that their dispositions should differ?

239

There are men whose mind (a faculty which can be applied universally) is only a sort of talent that seems to dominate them, which they're unable to control and which refuses to obey their common sense.

240

I'm tempted to say of metaphysicians what someone once said of the Basques: 'People claim they can understand each other but I'm absolutely convinced they can't.'

241

A little learning makes you despise erudition; you need a great deal to appreciate it properly.

242

A good number of works owe their success to the mediocrity of their authors' ideas, which match the mediocrity of those of the general public.

243

Middle-class women who have the hope or the urge to make their mark in high society don't enjoy the happiness that can be found either in nature or in

society; they are the most miserable creatures I've
ever met.

244

Good taste, tact and good form are more closely
related than people seem to think. Tact is good taste
applied to social behaviour and personal conduct;
good form is good taste in discussion and
conversation.

245

To produce great literature or at least bring about any
revolutionary change, you need, as in politics, to find
everything in a state of readiness, to be born at the
right time.

246

An author expressing himself, in what, in his
own opinion, is a very clear manner, is sometimes
found obscure by his readers. This is easy to explain:
the author is moving from his own ideas to his
expression of them, the reader from the expression
to the ideas.

247

In the fine arts and indeed in many other matters,

it is only the things you've never learned which you know really well.

248
People often feel annoyed by writers who retreat from society; they expect them to continue to show interest even though they gain little benefit from it; they've got to be present whenever lots are being drawn, even in a lottery for which they haven't got any tickets.

249
Having lots of ideas doesn't mean you're clever, any more than having lots of soldiers means you're a good general.

250
The things you know best are: first, those you know intuitively; second, those you've learned from experience; third, those you've learned not from but through books and the ideas they've inspired in you; and finally, those you've learned in books and from your teachers.

251
The memoirs of men who've held high office or of

men of letters (even those who've achieved very little) are written for posterity, thereby revealing their authors' secret vanity. They remind me of the story of the saint who is said to have left a hundred thousand crowns towards his own canonisation.

252

Economists are like surgeons who have two scalpels, one with a very sharp edge, the other with a very jagged edge; with the first, they do superb autopsies on the dead; with the other, they perform excruciating operations on the living.

253

A number of writers think they love fame, when what they really love is vanity, two very different things, indeed opposites: fame is a grand, vanity a petty, passion. The difference between them is as great as that between loving and womanising.

254

Most modern books strike one as having been dashed off in a single day – based on old books read the day before.

255

Paris, that gay city of enjoyment and pleasure, etc. –
where four-fifths of the population are dying in
distress.

256

Almost all history is a story of horror. If tyrants
condemn it during their lifetime, their successors
seem to allow the crimes of their predecessors to be
passed on to posterity, thereby diverting attention
from the horror they themselves inspire. Indeed,
there's hardly anything else to console ordinary
people except to teach them that their forebears
were equally miserable – or even more so.

257

In France, we leave arsonists in peace and persecute
those who sound the alarm.

258

It's most unfortunate that our character can deprive
us of the role in society which our talents rightfully
deserve.

259

Great men produce their masterpieces when passion

has died down, just as soil is more fertile after a volcanic eruption.

260

People are derided for their enthusiastic admiration of savage as opposed to civilised societies. But I'd like someone to answer this: we've never heard any cases of savages going mad, committing suicide or wanting to become part of any civilised community, whereas large numbers of settlers in the Cape of Good Hope, as well as in North and South America, after living for some time among the natives before returning home, have gone back to live in the wilds.

261

From the point of view of society, it's unfortunate for mankind that, although moral and political evil may be defined as harmful, it's not possible to define good as being useful, for what is useful at the moment may cause long-term, even irreparable, harm.

262

The net result of thirty or forty centuries of intellectual and physical effort has been to deliver three hundred million people all round the globe into the hands of some thirty or so despots, mainly ignorant idiots, each controlled by three or four stupid scoundrels. So what can we think of mankind? And what can we expect to see in the future?

263

In everything, there's a moment of ripeness which you have to watch and wait for. Happy the man who arrives at this crucial moment!

264

We must start human society again from scratch; as Francis Bacon said, we must recreate human understanding.

265

By outlawing suicide, kings and priests have tried to ensure that our slavery is never-ending. They want to keep us shut up in a dungeon without an exit, like that criminal archbishop in Dante who had the door of the wretched Ugolino's prison walled up.

266

Unfortunately for mankind – and perhaps fortunately for tyrants – the poor and downtrodden lack the instinct or pride of elephants who refuse to breed in captivity.

267

It's an indisputable fact that there are in France seven million people begging for alms and twelve million in no position to help them.

268

Most social institutions seem designed to keep people, intellectually and emotionally, in a state of mediocrity which makes them fitter to govern or be governed.

269

'We're the intermediary between the King and his subjects,' claim the nobility. Yes indeed – and the hound is the intermediary between the hunter and the hare.

270

The poor are the black slaves of Europe.

271

Reduce the people's burdens and you reduce its ferocity, just as you can restore a man's health with a good bowl of soup.

272

France is a country where it's often helpful to display

your vices and always dangerous to reveal your virtues.

273
Wealth, and the uniform that goes with it, turns life into a performance where, in the long run, the most decent of men has to play a part, whether he likes it or not.

274
One of the reasons why corporate bodies and assemblies are unable to produce much more than stupid results is that, in any public assembly, the strongest arguments for or against either the subject or the person under discussion can never be openly stated without running grave risks or stirring up powerful prejudices.

275
In their unshakeable determination to keep people in ignorance, theologians, together with their henchmen in government who are equally resolved to oppress them, make the gratuitous assumption that the great majority of people by reason of their purely mechanical, manual occupations are doomed to remain stupid. They imagine that artisans are

incapable of reaching the level of understanding necessary to assert their rights as men and as citizens. Wouldn't that lead you to think that such a level of understanding is extremely complicated? Yet if only one quarter of the time now devoted to numbing their powers of thought had been used to enlighten them and instead of stuffing their heads with an absurd catechism of incomprehensible metaphysics, they had been taught the basic principles of man's rights and of the duties based on those rights, we'd have been amazed to see how far they would have progressed along this path, which can be found in any decent elementary textbook. If, instead of preaching the doctrine of patience, suffering, abnegation and degradation, so helpful to usurpers, they had taught people how to recognise their rights and their duty to defend them, they would have recognised that nature, which has created man as a social animal, has supplied him with all the common sense required to form a society based on reason.

276
Success breeds success just as money breeds money.

277
Divorce is so natural a state that in a number of

households it sleeps every night between married couples.

278
Natural scientists say that amongst animal species, degeneration starts with the female. Moral scientists can apply the same observation to civilised society.

279
When the famous general Turenne was asked if he never felt his courage failing before a great battle, he replied: 'Yes, I do feel extremely alarmed, but in the army there are quite a number of subordinate officers and large numbers of ordinary soldiers who don't.'

280
My miserable experiences as a young man provided me with a protective armour against all those that came later.

281
Everyone who's risen from the lower classes of society conspires with all the others to oppress them; from the man who joins the militia to the businessman who becomes a state secretary, the preacher who

leaves his village to preach the need to submit to arbitrary authority, middle-class royal historiographers, etc. They're like the soldiers of Cadmus: the first ones to obtain arms turn against their fellow soldiers.

282

He has an imagination which, as soon as he loses an illusion, creates another one, like those roses that flower all the year round.

283

Clumsy benefactors have been compared to a goat which, after allowing herself to be milked, kicks over the jar containing her own milk.

284

You don't clean out the stables of Augeas with a feather duster.

285

A pretty woman noticed that her lover was sulky and showing signs of behaving like a husband. She said: 'I hope you understand that in public, when you're in the same room as my husband, it's good manners to be more agreeable than he is.'

286

A lover saw his mistress flirting with her husband; he left the room exclaiming: 'Good God! That really is the limit! How can you be so shameless?'

287

About to launch an attack on a woman and realising he wasn't quite ready, a man said: 'Would you mind waiting for a quarter of an hour before losing your virtue?'

288

Writers, particularly poets, are like peacocks; you toss them a few niggardly grains of corn in their cage and bring them out now and then to display their tails; meanwhile cocks and hens, ducks and turkeys walk around freely in the farmyard, happily filling their crops.

289

Infuriated by the *Système de la nature* of Baron d'Holbach, a learned doctor of the Sorbonne exclaimed: 'It's an abomination, an utterly execrable work, an irrefutable proof of atheism!'

290

A woman said: 'M... was passionately in love with me and thought he was being sensible. I was madly infatuated but suspected it, so from that point of view I was more sensible than he was.'

291

At the wedding of a seventy-year-old man to a girl of seventeen, the priest took as his text: 'Father, forgive them, for they know not what they do.'

292

A man said casually to a friend: 'This morning we condemned three men to death; two of them were certainly guilty.'

293

The tyranny of keeping up with fashion is a very queer thing: a gentleman was separated from his wife, whom he neither loved nor admired. Hearing she had smallpox, he went back to her, caught the disease and died, leaving her a vast fortune, with permission to remarry.

294

Men are so perverse that any hope or desire to reform

them, to see them turn into decent, reasonable beings is an absurdly romantic notion, forgivable only in the very young and innocent.

295
M..., an inveterate bachelor, used to say jokingly that marriage was too perfect a state for imperfect man.

296
People with great qualities sometimes suffer from false modesty which leads them to spend their lives in relative obscurity. I'm reminded of a remark made at a luncheon where members of Court circles were present, by a man universally recognised for his eminence: 'Ah, gentlemen, how bitterly I regret the time I wasted before I realised how superior I am to all of you!'

297
There's an Italian proverb which says: 'There's no truth and no religion below the navel.'

298
Speaking of a former friend who'd renewed his friendship after he'd noticed his situation had improved, he wittily remarked: 'He not only likes

his friends to be doing well, he insists on it.'

299

M... said: 'I do everything I can to have a good opinion of everyone yet I still find there are very few people I have a good opinion of. I just can't understand it.'

300

M.... would say to me: 'I've restricted myself to finding all my pleasures within myself, that is to say, relying solely on my own intelligence. Nature has placed in a man's brain a small gland called the cerebellum which acts as a mirror. In it he can see, more or less, on a large or small scale, either in detail or in general, every object in the universe and even the products of his own mind. It's his private magic lantern, showing scenes in which he is both actor and spectator. This is a man's real domain and it marks the limits of his powers. Anything else is beyond his reach.'

301

Diderot made the comment that a writer can have a mistress who produces books but needs a wife who can produce a shirt.

302

'Today I performed a rather unusual act of kindness,' said M…. 'I was able to console a decent, honourable man, with many excellent qualities and an income of 100,000 francs a year, who bears a very distinguished name, is extremely intelligent and healthy, etc. And I myself am poor, obscure and in very bad health.'

303

Someone suggested to Louis XIV that he ought to take a very grand lady, whose name I forget, as his mistress. He refused, saying she'd cost too much to get rid of.

304

For thirty years a man had been visiting the same lady every evening. His wife died and everyone thought he'd marry her and encouraged him to do so. He refused, saying: 'Where could I spend my evenings?'

305

A man with a very promiscuous wife used to sleep once a month in her bedroom to avoid any risk of scandal should she become pregnant. He'd then leave, saying: 'Well that's that, the field's now free for all comers.'

306

People were challenging M...'s view of a work, pointing out that the public thought differently. 'The public? The public?' he exclaimed. 'How many idiots does it take to form public opinion?'

307

'In the very best society,' M... said, 'all I found was indigestible luncheons, dull dinners, crafty conversations, acquaintances but no friends, copulations but no love.'

308

After reading St Jerome's lively account of his passions, M... said: 'I'm more impressed by the violence of his feelings than frightened by his penance.'

309

A man completely indifferent towards life said as he was dying: 'This is going to make my doctor feel very silly!'

310

M... used to say that since any decent, clear-sighted man who saw society in its true light couldn't fail to feel bitter, it was absolutely essential to see the funny side of things, to adopt the habit of viewing men as puppets and society as a stage on which they strut around. Then everything would look different: the beliefs of the various classes of society, the vanity at the heart of all of them, their particular forms of pettiness, their various ways of cheating and so on would all become a source of amusement and help you to retain your sanity.

311
M… said: 'I've just dropped two friends, one because he never talked to me about himself, the other because he never talked to me about myself.'

312
A man was walking around dressed in deep mourning from head to foot – black wig, long face, hired mourners. One of his friends enquired sympathetically who it was he'd lost: 'Lost?' the man retorted. 'I haven't lost anything. I've just been widowed.'

313
Madame de C. said to M.B.: 'What I love about you is…'

'Ah, Madame,' he exclaimed frantically, 'if you know that, I'm lost...!'

314

M..., a Provençal and full of rather whimsical ideas, was talking to me about kings and their ministers and remarked that once the system had been properly set up, the choice of any particular minister was irrelevant. 'It's like dogs turning a spit,' he said. 'All they need do is to keep their paws moving, their pedigree's unimportant, they don't need to be clever or have a good nose, the spit goes on turning and the meal will be more or less edible.'

315

You must pander to a man's tastes or threaten his sense of security: they're monkeys who'll dance for their nuts or for fear of a thrashing.

316

The Duke of Marlborough was once in a trench with a friend and his nephew when his friend was struck in the head by a cannonball which spattered his brains over his nephew's face, causing him to recoil in horror. Quite unmoved, the Duke asked him why he seemed so upset. 'Yes, I am indeed upset,' the nephew replied, wiping his face. 'I'm amazed that a man with so much brain should, of his own accord, expose himself unnecessarily to so much danger.'

317

M..., well-known for his social qualities, told me that he owed this reputation largely to his willingness, when required, to go to bed with women of forty and listen to the talk of old men of eighty.

318

M... was talking about life and how things were going from bad to worse. 'I once read,' he said, 'that there's nothing worse for everyone concerned than a reign that's lasted too long. I've also heard that God is eternal. Need we say more?'

319

M... made a very shrewd and discerning comment: 'However tiresome the faults of the people with whom we associate, and however alien to our own true nature these faults may be, we're bound to acquire some of them ourselves – even if we suffer as a result.'

320

In the course of a philosophical discussion, M… said to M.L.: 'Few things and few people interest me, and myself least of all.'

'Aren't those two much the same thing?' replied M.L. 'Aren't they just cause and effect?'

'True enough,' retorted M… drily, 'but I'm merely stating a fact: it gradually dawned on me that the longer you live and see what men are like, the more you have to choose between being either broken-hearted or stony-hearted.'

321

La Fontaine was listening to people deploring the fate of those condemned to hell-fire for all eternity. 'My own opinion,' he said, 'is that they very quickly settle in and take to it like ducks to water.'

322

M… thought honourable men were very hard to find in society: 'They're a sub-variety of the human race,' he said.

323

A very boring man attracted many guests to his house because he offered excellent food and drink. M…

commented: 'He's extremely edible – and quite indigestible.'

324

People were sympathising with a man who'd spent some time in the country for the company he'd had to keep. 'You're quite wrong,' he said, 'the good company was the same as everywhere else and the bad company was really excellent.'

325

A man, overjoyed at the thought of his marriage to a charming young woman, said to his future brother-in-law: 'I'm the luckiest man in the world.'

'That depends.'

'What do you mean, 'that depends'?'

'It depends on what her first lover's like.'

326

Asked why pleasures left him cold, M… replied: 'It's not through lack of feeling but they all seem to me overrated. Fame exposes you to slander; winning anyone's respect requires endless effort; enjoyment involves constant care and attention as well as considerable physical exertion. Society is full of pitfalls: everything you do is analysed and judged.

The very best society offers nothing I can't find in myself. As a result of all these experiences, without becoming either apathetic or indifferent, I've reached a state of inertia where any situation I happen to be in seems the best because it's stable. Love is a source of worry, pleasure without love lasts only a few minutes; marriage is even more closely scrutinised and criticised than anything else; the privilege of fatherhood can lead to one disaster after another. And running a house should be left to innkeepers. People's motives for making your acquaintance are blatant self-interest and can only deceive someone stupid or flatter someone ridiculously vain. I've come to the conclusion that the only worthwhile thing for anyone no longer interested in futile activities is to preserve their own peace of mind and enjoy friendship and quiet meditation.'

327

Intrigued by his character, I've been observing M... closely: a very likeable man with no desire to be liked except by his friends and people he respects; on the other hand, anxious never to give offence – a most sensible attitude which shows proper concern for both friendship and society. It's possible to do more good than he does, but no one will ever do less harm; to be more anxious to help, but never less ready to interfere; to be more gentle, but never less likely to cause hurt.

328

M… used to remark that aristocratic society was like a bawdy house which you weren't ashamed to admit visiting.

329

Asked why he'd stopped going into society, M.N. replied: 'The fact is that I'm no longer interested in women and I've discovered what men are like.'

330

During his last illness, Prince de Conti said to Beaumarchais that after all the hardships of war and the ravages caused by wine and women, he could hardly expect to recover. 'Well, as far as war's concerned,' Beaumarchais replied, 'Prince Eugene fought twenty campaigns and died aged seventy-eight; as for wine, the Marquis de Brancas used to drink six bottles of champagne a day and lived to eighty-four.'

'Yes, but what about all my love affairs?' the prince asked.

'Your dear mother...?' murmured Beaumarchais.
(She had died at the age of seventy-nine.)

'You're right!' exclaimed Conti. 'I still stand a chance.'

331

Louis XV said to one of his mistresses: 'You've been to bed with all my subjects.'

'Oh, Your Majesty!'

'You had the Duc de Choiseul.'

'He's so powerful...'

'Maréchal de Richelieu.'

'He's so witty...'

'Manville.'

'He has such lovely legs...'

'And what about the Duc d'Aumont, who hasn't got any of these fine qualities?'

'Oh sire, he's so devoted to Your Majesty!'

332

Posterity merely consists of the opinion of a series of publics; and just look at today's!

333

A woman was describing a man: 'He's a decent sort, a trifle touchy; rather like a fresh-water perch – white flesh, wholesome, not much flavour and full of bones.'

334

I once knew a misanthrope who, when in a good
mood, would say that he'd not be too surprised if,
unknown to anyone, in some remote corner, there
mightn't be a decent honest man hidden away,
somewhere or other.

335

A man was drinking an excellent wine and made no
comment on it. His host then served him some very
ordinary wine. 'That's quite a nice wine,' commented
the unforthcoming guest. 'It's the cheapest I could get
and the first one was absolute nectar of the gods.'

'Of course it was,' replied his friend, 'that's why I
didn't praise it. This is the one that needs support.'

336

I was talking the other day to a man who seemed
completely without illusions on the subject of women,
at an age when it's still permissible to have kept a few.
When I expressed surprise at his indifference, he
replied solemnly: 'A man can't turn back the pages
of his life. In my day, like everyone else, I've been
the lover of a tart, the victim of a flirt, a stopgap

for a slut and tricked by an intriguer. What's left?'

'Friendship with a woman of real feeling?'

'Well, if you want to move into the realm of fiction...'

337

'Please believe me,' said M... to a very rich man. 'I've absolutely no need of anything I haven't got.'

338

Talking about a girl who wasn't in the slightest degree mercenary and who always remained faithful to the men she'd chosen, M... said: 'She's a charming young woman who lives as decent a life as anyone can who doesn't feel attracted to either matrimony or chastity.'

339

My neighbour at table asked me whether the woman opposite us was the wife of the man beside her. I'd noticed that they hadn't exchanged a single word. I replied: 'Either he doesn't know her or she's his wife.'

340

A philosopher said to me that, having examined the social and political organisation of society, he now

confined his studies to travel books about savages
or to the ordinary daily lives of children.

341

I've forgotten who it was[11] who said he'd like to live
to see the last king strangled with the guts of the last
priest.

342

They were trying to persuade M... to talk about
public and private abuses. He replied stiffly: 'Every
day I add to the list of things I refuse to discuss. The
wiser the man, the longer the list.'

343

'In society,' M... would say, 'you have three sorts of
friends: those who like you, those who couldn't care
less about you, and those who hate you.'

344

M... said: 'I can't imagine why Mme L. is so keen for
me to call on her, because the longer I stay away, the
less I despise her. And the same applies to society in
general.'

345

Someone asked a bishop to lend him his house in the country, which he never went to himself. The bishop said: 'Don't you know that we must always have a place where we never go but where we think we'd be happy if we did?' The man thought for a moment and replied: 'You're right. And that's the reason why people find the idea of paradise so attractive.'

346

'One day,' said M..., 'after leaving a National Assembly presided over by a Jew, I hope to go on to attend the wedding of a Roman Catholic divorced from his first wife, a Lutheran, and who's marrying a young Anabaptist; and afterwards on to the wedding reception with a priest who'll introduce me to his young Anglican wife, whom he's married after being widowed by the death of his first wife, a Calvinist.'

347

'What makes society so disagreeable,' someone remarked to me, 'is, firstly, the rogues, and, secondly, the decent people, so in order to make it relatively tolerable, you'd have to eliminate the former and reform the latter. In other words, we need to abolish hell and improve paradise.'

348

A misanthrope, notorious for avoiding other people's company, used to say: 'How terribly fond you have to be of someone to want to go and call on them.'

349

A highly intelligent man, asked why he hadn't been seen during the Revolution, said: 'The truth is that over the last thirty years I've found people so unpleasant, privately and in general, that I didn't hope for much good to come out of them publicly and collectively.'

350

A decree was passed requiring all artillery officers to be of noble birth and, since artillery officers need to be intelligent, a most amusing situation arose: in the examinations to select such officers, the most intelligent candidates were commoners, and as an official genealogist checked all their pedigrees, the result was that, out of a hundred or so cadets, only four or five turned out to be both intelligent and noble.

351

During a discussion on the pleasures of love, a man

told me that once you've discovered that you're no longer inexhaustible, you have to be extremely careful, rather like people living in reduced circumstances after being very rich. 'As for myself,' he added, ' as soon as I found I had to choose between signing a bill payable on sight and a promissory note, I gave up banking.'

352

M... was being criticised for his attitude towards women. 'What I say about women,' he replied, 'is what one of them once said to me about children: "I have in my mind a son whom I was unable to bring into the world." And in my own mind I see a woman, of a very rare kind, and that woman protects me from the more numerous sort. How grateful I am to her!'

353

Someone was talking about the respect we owe the public. 'Yes,' said M.... 'It's a question of prudence. Nobody has a high opinion of fishwives but who'd dare offend them when they're walking through the fish-market?'

354

A man had been visiting a lady regularly every day

and the rumour was spreading that he was going to
marry her. He said to one of his friends: 'There are
few men she'd be less likely to marry and the same
thing applies to me: it'd be very odd if, in the
course of a friendship of more than fifteen years, we
hadn't come to realise how extremely antipathetic we
are.'

355
A man rejected a woman's advances. 'What's the
point of being intelligent if it doesn't enable you to
turn down that woman?' he said.

356
'If I am anything to go by,' M... said, 'man is a
foolish animal.'

357
To describe his contempt for someone, M... had a
pet expression: 'He's next to the lowest of the low.'
Asked why he didn't say 'the lowest', he replied:
'Because I don't want to discourage anyone. There's
a very long queue.'

358
M... was being admonished for his unsociability. 'It's

because I'm more used to my own shortcomings than anyone else's,' he replied.

359

M... was telling me that the following principles had always proved useful in his relations with women: 'Always talk about them in general terms; praise the nice ones, keep quiet about the others; don't see too much of them; never trust them; and never let your happiness depend on only one of them, whoever she may be.'

360

Someone remarked to a doctor who practised Mesmer's methods: 'Well, despite all your claims, your patient died.' The doctor replied: 'Ah, but you didn't see my full course of treatment – my patient died cured.'

361

'You're yawning,' a wife said to her husband. 'Ah, my dear,' he replied, 'don't you know that husband and wife are one flesh – and when I'm alone, I get bored.'

362

People were surprised to see a lady watching a

tragedy and not crying. 'Oh, nothing would have pleased me better,' she said, 'but I happen to be dining out tonight and I don't want to smudge my make-up.'

363
A devout and naïve Christian was admonishing those who questioned the articles of faith. 'A true Christian must never examine the things he's told to believe, gentlemen,' he said. 'It's like taking a pill: if you chew it, it's so bitter you'll never get it down.'

364
'I prefer the company of atheists to that of believers,' a man said. 'When I'm with an atheist, all the half-proofs of God's existence come to mind and when I'm with a believer all the half-proofs against Him come flooding back...'

365
'Happiness is not easy to find,' M... would say. 'It's very difficult to find it in yourself – and impossible to find anywhere else.'

366
A doctor was being accused of always predicting the

worst. 'It's because I've attended so many funerals of patients of my optimistic colleagues,' he explained. 'At least, if mine die, I can't be accused of being stupid.'

367

A man visiting an actress who'd just been rather publicly abandoned by her lover was surprised to find her playing her harp. 'I thought I'd find you devastated,' he said. 'Yes, indeed,' replied the actress. 'You should have seen me yesterday.'

368

Faced by an awkward question, M... said: 'That's exactly the sort of thing I know perfectly well when no one's talking about it and as soon as I'm asked, it goes completely out of my head.'

369

A man professing to have a high opinion of women was asked if he'd had many. 'Not half as many as I would have had if I thought badly of them,' he replied.

370

There's an Italian farce on the shortcomings of both

sexes, in which Harlequin remarks that we'd all be perfect if only we were neither men nor women.

371

M... used to say: 'I'm not greatly bothered about being a Christian but I wouldn't object to being able to believe in God.'

372

The politician Charles James Fox had borrowed vast sums of money from various Jews in the expectation of a legacy from an uncle. The uncle married and had a son. 'That young man's a Messiah,' commented Fox. 'He's been born to destroy the Jews.'

373

A country doctor visiting a patient in a neighbouring village took a gun in case he saw some game on the way. He met a farmer who asked where he was going.

'Visiting a patient.'

'Afraid he'll get away, eh?'

374

Having received some services from a French nobleman, the Pope asked if he could return the compliment. The wily baron asked if it would be possible to let him have some relics of a saint. Though surprised by such a request from a Frenchman, the Pope arranged to let him have some. The baron had a small estate in the Pyrenees which had no outlet for its produce and thus returned very small revenues. A shrine was built and the news was spread around. Visitors came swarming in; miracles were performed, the local population grew, the price of their produce rose... and the baron's revenues tripled.

375

A poet asked M... his opinion of one of his couplets. 'Superb,' replied M.... 'A bit long here and there, perhaps?'

376

A man was boasting: 'I've only ever committed one bad action in my whole life.'

'And when's it going to end?' enquired M....

377

An *abbé* asked the Duke of Orleans to grant him an abbey. 'Oh, get fucked,' the duke replied, not bothering to look up. 'But you need money even for that, as Your Highness will observe if he will deign to look.' The *abbé* was hideously ugly. The Regent burst out laughing and the *abbé* got his abbey.

378

'Whenever a temptation comes my way,' said M... 'do you know what I do with it?'

'No.'

'I hang on to it.'

379

A little boy was asking his mother for some candied fruit. 'Give me too much,' he said.

380

Meeting a cardinal who'd been presiding over a Church Assembly, a priest noticed that he was in a foul temper and asked the reason. 'Reason? Reason?' exclaimed the cardinal. 'Every possible reason. I've never seen a more disastrous Assembly. Can you imagine: even the youngest priests refused to be fobbed off by bad arguments!'

381

During a heated discussion in the French Academy, a member said: 'Gentlemen, suppose we agree not to speak more than four at a time?'

382

Madame de Tencin said that many very clever people made social blunders because they could never believe that society was quite as stupid as it really was.

383

In the course of a fanatical address to the King condemning Protestants, a bishop claimed to be speaking on behalf of the clergy. A fellow bishop asked him why he had spoken on their behalf without consulting them. 'I consulted my crucifix,' he replied. 'In that case,' the other bishop observed, 'why didn't you quote the exact words of your crucifix's reply?'

384

Urged on by her father, a grain merchant, one of the Regent's mistesses had established a wheat monopoly which had reduced the population to misery and finally led to an uprising which a company of musketeers was sent to suppress. Its commander was given the order: 'Shoot the scum!' This is how the officer concerned, a decent man with scruples about firing on his fellow countrymen, interpreted his instructions: he told the company to load, then walked out in front, holding his hat in one hand and his orders in the other. 'Gentlemen,' he said, 'I have here orders to shoot the scum. I ask all those who aren't scum to withdraw before I fire.' Everybody hastily disappeared.

385

A man had just lost a lawsuit that had been going on for twenty years and people were sympathising with him for the worry it must have caused him, only to lose it. 'True,' the man replied, 'but for twenty years, every night, I won it.' It was the reply of a true philosopher and one which can be applied in all kinds of cases. It explains why men like flirts: for six months she lets you think you're going to have her and when you don't succeed, it's only for one night.

386

D'Alembert, an outstanding mathematician, was talking to a very eminent Swiss jurist who was saying how much he admired the universality of Voltaire's genius; it was only in his knowledge of civil law that he seemed to have certain gaps. 'Yes,' said d'Alembert. 'And I found him a little weak only in his grasp of geometry.'

387

The Archbishop of Toulouse gave a nobleman

a handsome gratuity for special services to the province. His main service had been to go to bed with the archbishop's old and ugly mother.

388

'Why do people talk such a lot about learning how to die?' enquired a fourteen-year-old girl. 'It seems to me everybody does it perfectly well the first time.'

389

A man was violently criticising a recent tragedy. 'But the man whose box you were sharing says that tears were running down your cheeks.' 'That's quite probable,' replied the critic, 'but when I saw him starting to cry at the very first scene, I thought it was only polite to share his grief.'

390

Voltaire was staying with Madame du Châtelet and sitting in her bedroom with a little boy on his lap, chatting with him about life, he said: 'To be successful with men, you must always have the ladies on your side and in order to do that you have to know what they're like. Well, you'll discover that all women are false and faithless.' 'What do you mean, all women?

What do you think you're telling him?' exclaimed
Madame du Châtelet furiously. 'Ah, madame, we
must never lie to children,' Voltaire replied.

391
A gentleman who spent a great deal of time in
society and knew it intimately said that before leaving
every morning you ought to eat a toad in order to
ensure you won't have anything more disgusting to
do during the day.

392
An impoverished man who'd written a book
attacking the government was complaining: 'What
the devil's happened? What are they waiting for?
Not a word from the Bastille and here I am with my
rent to pay any day now; if they don't hurry up and
take me in quickly, I don't know what I shall do!'

393
'In spite of all the jokes about marriage,' said M...,
'I can't see what anyone can say against a man of
sixty who marries a woman of fifty-six.'

394
A man who lacks adaptability at times when it's in his

interest to show it invariably ends up isolated with only that abstract quality called Virtue as his friend, and she'll let him starve.

395
Anyone who's not a misanthrope by the time he's forty has never felt the slightest affection for the human race.

396
It seems to me that, assuming that they're both equally discerning and intelligent, a man born rich will never know nature, society or the human heart as well as the man who's poor. The fact is that where the rich man was enjoying himself, the poor man was finding consolation in thought.

397
It's pointless to try to make people better by proving that they're beyond all hope of redemption.

398
'I'd like to propose,' a man said, 'the following pact with scandalmongers and various other types of scoundrel: I'm perfectly willing to be slandered so long as, by one single act, even done by mistake or

in a good cause, I've provided some evidence for the slander, so long as the slander isn't mere embroidery and the facts and circumstancs aren't pure fabrication, in a word, if the slander has sum and substance. And to the other scoundrels I'd say: I've no objection to being treated badly as long as the person doing it is motivated by self-interest and is not, as is often the case, doing it for the sheer fun of it.'

399
I asked M... why he'd turned down the offer of a particular post. 'I didn't want a post where the office is more important than the holder of it,' he replied.

400
A misanthrope who was something of a wag used to say, in reference to the general nastiness of mankind: 'The only reason why God has refrained from sending a second Flood is because the first one proved such a failure.'

401
M. de R. used to be less harsh, less abrasive than he is now; he's used up almost his whole stock of forbearance and the little that's left he keeps for himself.

402

M... was accused of disliking everybody. 'Not at all,' he said. 'I was once on the point of doing so but I took steps to remedy it.'

'What did you do?'

'I stopped having anything to do with anybody.'

403

On the subject of women M... once said jokingly: 'You have to choose either to love them or to know them. There's no middle course.'

404

'It's about time,' said M..., 'for philosophers to draw up a list of prohibited works, on the lines of the Inquisition in Rome and Madrid; but their list needs to be even longer. And even in the books they approve of in general, how many particular ideas would they have to condemn as being immoral or just plain silly?'

405

M. de Calonne was about to show some ladies round his study and having difficulty in finding the keyhole, he exclaimed: 'Fuck it!' Realising what he'd said, he turned to them and added: 'My apologies, ladies. But in my life, I've done a great variety of things and I have discovered that there's only one word that's absolutely infallible.' The key went straight into the lock.

406

I asked M... why he'd rejected the chance of a very advantageous marriage. He replied: 'I don't want to marry because I'm afraid I might have a son like myself.' Seeing my surprise, for he himself is a very pleasant, decent man, he added: 'Yes, afraid of having a son who'd be poor like his father, who wouldn't know how to lie, flatter or grovel, and would have to endure the same hardships as I have.'

407

Apart from deliberately evil or criminal acts, you must never forget the harm caused by (i) good intentions and good deeds which have bad effects on society in general, such as tolerating wrongdoing or the foolishness of being too forgiving; (ii) the problems caused by applying philosophy inappropriately or tactlessness when offering help to friends; (iii) applying sensible, useful maxims at the wrong time and place.

408

'When you see how disgustingly our government, our justice and our meals are dished up,' said a witty lawyer, 'it's really enough to turn your stomach.'

409

M. de L. was trying to discourage a recently widowed lady from remarrying: 'Just think how privileged you are to bear the name of a man who can never do anything foolish any more,' he said.

410

A certain viscount went over to a man and said: 'Is it true, sir, that in a salon where people had been kind enough to say that I was witty, you asserted that I was not?' The man replied: 'Sir, there's not one word of truth in that whole story. I've never been in any salon where you were described as witty and I've never had the opportunity of stating that you weren't.'

411

A lady noticed that instead of paying attention to her, Maréchal de Richelieu was eyeing a woman who was extremely beautiful but had the reputation of being a bit dim.'

'Ah, *Maréchal*,' she said, 'I can see you're by no means short-sighted but I suspect you of being somewhat hard of hearing.'

412

A man begins every stage of his life as a novice.

413

M... said of a lady who was trying hard to become deeply religious that it was a hopeless task because, quite apart from the foolishness needed to become a believer, in order to achieve salvation you had to display at all times a fundamental stupidity which she would often find impossible. He added: 'They call this stupidity grace.'

414

A woman had just lost her husband. Next day, her confessor called to console her and found her playing cards with a smartly dressed young man. Seeing his bewilderment, she said: 'Only half an hour ago, I was crying my heart out... but then I bet my grief against this young man... and he won.'

415

An eccentric English lord got drunk in an inn, killed

one of the servants and went away quite unaware of what he'd done. The distraught landlord went round to his house to tell him what had happened. 'Oh, put him on my bill,' the lord stammered.

416

Once when her son had been particularly wilful, his mother complained: 'Children are so selfish!'

'Yes,' remarked M..., 'and then they learn manners.'

417

Fontenelle was dying and a friend called to see him. 'How are you coming on?' he asked. 'I'm not,' replied Fontenelle. 'I'm going off.'

418

When Fontenelle was ninety-five, a ninety-year-old lady said to him: 'God seems to have forgotten us.'

'Shush,' he replied, placing his fingers on her lips.

419

M... was talking about his constant refusal to lead a sensible life and the pleasures he indulged in, which were the only reasons preventing him from recovering his health. 'If it wasn't for me,' he said, 'I'd be as fit as a fiddle.'

420

A priest was stealing little gold hearts and other offerings from his church. When brought to justice, he claimed that they were gifts from the Virgin Mary. He was condemned and, as was customary, the sentence went to the King of Prussia for ratification. Frederick called a council of theologians to decide whether it was strictly impossible for the Virgin to make such small gifts to a devout Catholic. Greatly embarrassed, the theologians ruled that it was not strictly impossible. The King wrote at the bottom of the guilty priest's sentence: 'I remit this sentence but I forbid this priest, under pain of death, to accept further gifts of any sort from the Virgin or from any other of the saints.'

421

Passing through Soissons, Voltaire received a deputation of members of the local Academy, which they described as the elder daughter of the French Academy. 'Yes, indeed,' Voltaire replied, 'an elder daughter of spotless reputation, a very proper young lady who's never drawn attention to herself.'

422

One of M...'s friends was complaining to him that he felt that he mistrusted him. 'After all,' he said, 'you're not rich and you seem to have forgotten that I'm your friend.'

'All right then, I promise to borrow twenty-five louis from you as soon as you've paid off all your debts,' M... replied.

423

A man was very reluctant to accept the last sacraments. 'I'll pretend I'm not dead,' he said.

424

Fox, an inveterate gambler, used to say there were two great pleasures in gambling – one was winning, the other was losing.

425

A man well-known to be a liar had just told a most improbable story. 'Sir, while I believe you,' someone said, 'you must admit that it's very wrong of truth not to condescend to be more plausible.'

426

Maréchal de Luxembourg was held for two years

in the Bastille accused of being involved in magical practices. He was then released and given command of an army. 'I see they still need a bit of magic,' he remarked with a smile.

427

An old man I once knew in my youth said to me: 'I've almost invariably seen the careers of successful ministers and favourites end in such a way that made them envy their officials and secretaries.'

428

Seeing her mother devastated at losing her position at Court, her nine-year-old daughter said to her: 'Mummy, why do you enjoy being bored to death?'

429

In the course of a battle, an Irish soldier was claiming to have taken a prisoner. He called out to one of his comrades: 'He's refusing to come with me.'

'Well, let him go then.'

' But he's refusing to go away,' replied the Irishman.

430

I commented to M... that he had a very young and

pretty housekeeper. 'Differences in age are quite immaterial,' he replied naïvely, 'it's compatibility of character that counts.'

431

A man met a grave-digger to whom he owed money for burying his daughter and offered to pay him. 'No hurry, sir,' the grave-digger replied. 'One of your servants is ill and your wife doesn't look too good.'

432

M... used to say that at sessions of the French Academy you should never bother to read anything more than was strictly laid down in the statutes. 'When something's pointless,' he said, 'just confine yourself to what's unavoidable.'

433

At a time when new taxes aimed at the very rich were being introduced, a millionaire, one of a group of wealthy men who were complaining, was heard to say: 'These days, who can afford to be happy? Nobody but a few poor wretches!'

434

It's said that Rousseau 'had' the Comtesse de
Boufflers but (if you'll pardon the expression) failed
to get it up, thereby creating a great deal of ill-will
between the two. Once, in their presence, people were
saying that a love of mankind prevented you from
loving your own country. 'Speaking for myself,' said
Madame de Boufflers, 'that's not true. I'm a good
Frenchwoman but that doesn't stop me from being
concerned for the rest of mankind.'

'I see what you mean,' said Rousseau. 'Your top
half is French and the rest of you is cosmopolitan.'

435

While playing with one of her maids, Louis XVI's
daughter looked at her hand, counted up the number
of her fingers and exclaimed in astonishment:
'Goodness me, you've got the same number of fingers
as I have!' And she counted them once again, to make
sure.

436

Somebody said to John Donne: 'You must condemn
the sin but forgive the sinner.'

'What?' he exclaimed, 'Blame the cards and
absolve the card-sharpers?!'

437

During sessions of the French Academy, Duclos didn't hesitate to use expressions such as 'Fuck!' and 'Bugger!' One member, an *abbé* who because of his long face was nicknamed the 'great non-venomous snake', said to him: 'May I remind you that when the Academy's in official session, only words included in our Dictionary should be used?'

438

A man, himself not well-off, arranged to help an unfortunate person who had been unsuccessfully recommended to a lord and to a Farmer-General for help. When I gave him the full details of these two failed attempts, which made their conduct even more despicable, he replied calmly: 'How do you imagine the world would go on existing if the poor didn't continue to do the good which remedies the bad caused by the rich who show no signs of doing anything at all?'

439

'My enemies can never harm me,' M... would say, 'since they can't stop me from thinking and doing the decent thing.'

440

Referring to the ludicrous stupidity of ministers, M... used to say: 'If it weren't for the government, there'd be nothing to laugh at these days.'

441

I was told about this action of a nobleman which was so atrocious that I thought it must have been invented. His cook, serving in the army, had been caught looting. When he heard about it, he said: 'I'm very satisfied with my cook but I have a kitchen boy who's hopeless.' He sent for the young lad and gave him a letter to take to the Provost Marshal. The unfortunate young man did as he was told, was arrested and, still protesting his innocence, hanged.

442

M... had noticed that public opinion had been very influential in several important political decisions, such as appointments of ministers and high officials. He was hoping to help a friend in his career and said to M. de L.: 'Can't you whip up a little public opinion for him?'

443

Anyone who spends much time in high society

convinces me that he lacks feeling; I can't find anything there to appeal to the heart, or, indeed, anything that fails to make one heartless.

444

The ridiculous vanity of the bourgeoisie makes their daughters a rich source of manure for fertilising the estates of the nobility.

445

Too great a superiority can make a man unsuitable for society. You don't go to market with gold bullion in your pockets; you need small cash, a few silver and copper coins.

446

Society – clubs, salons, so-called high society – is a poor play, a bad, boring opera, made slightly better by its staging, costumes, and scenery.

447

In society, to prevent anyone taking advantage of him, the most modest man must put on a show of confidence; he's forced to call on his pride to protect his modesty.

448

M... used to say that what he liked most was peace, silence and obscurity. 'You've just described a sick-room,' someone said.

449

Many men are saved from becoming misanthropes by their weakness of character and lack of ideas, in a word by everything that stops us from living on our own.

450

Is it absolutely certain that a completely, genuinely rational man with an unimpeachable moral sense could live with anyone? By 'live' I don't mean co-exist without coming to blows. I mean enjoying each other's company, liking each other, taking pleasure in their dealings with each other.

451

When I was young, urged on by certain passions to go into society and forced to find relief for my troubles in the pleasures it offered, people continually lectured me on the delights of withdrawing from it and used to bore me to tears with their tedious sermons on the subject. At forty, having said goodbye to those passions which make society bearable, having seen how miserably futile it is and having no further need for high society to escape from hardships which had ceased to exist, I developed a taste for work and privacy which replaced all the rest. I avoided going into society, since which time people have never stopped pestering me to return. I've been accused of being a misanthrope and everything else. What can one make of this extraordinary change of mind? It's just that people feel the need to find fault with everything all the time.

452

People are now governed in the way they want. They've won the right to think – and ministers to act – foolishly.

453

A fanatical admirer of aristocatic privilege, having observed that the precincts of the Palace of Versailles were stinking with urine, ordered his servants and tenants to relieve themselves around his own château.

454

M... said that for marriage they should have adopted the same principle that applies to houses, where you can sign a lease for three, six or eight years, with the option to purchase if you find it suitable.

455

Madame de Tencin was gentle-mannered but quite unscrupulous, capable of absolutely anything. On one occasion people were praising the gentleness of her nature. 'Yes,' an *abbé* commented, 'if it was in her interest to poison you, I'm sure she'd choose the pleasantest poison possible.'

456

By making life often unendurable yet irresistibly attractive, nature seems to have treated mankind like an arsonist who sets fire to your house after posting guards at the door. Things have to become extremely dangerous before you feel forced to escape by jumping out of the window.

457

'I don't like,' M... used to say, 'impeccable, supremely virtuous women, with no weaknesses whatsoever. I can read over their door the words Dante put over the entrance to his Inferno: "All hope abandon, ye who enter here." It's the motto of the damned.'

458

Philosophers discover what virtues are of benefit, morally and politically; orators bring them to people's notice; but it's poets who make them really popular.

LITTLE
PHILOSOPHICAL
DIALOGUES

I

A - You've stopped seeing M...?

B - Yes, it became impossible.

A - How was that?

B - As long as only his morals were bad, I was able to go on seeing him but once he started keeping bad company there was no way I could continue.

II

A - We've fallen out with each other.

B - Why?

A - I made some uncomplimentary remarks about her.

B - I'm sure I can persuade her to make it up. What was it you said?

A - I called her a flirt.

B - That's all right.

A - And that she wasn't particularly pretty.

B - I wash my hands of it.

III

A - Would you believe it: I saw Madame de C. openly expressing her sorrow at the loss of her friend Monsieur F. in front of at least fifteen people?

B - Didn't I tell you she was a woman who'd stop at nothing to get what she wanted?

IV

The Cook - I couldn't get the salmon.

The Doctor of the Sorbonne - Why not?

The Cook - There was a councillor after it.

The Doctor - Here's a hundred crowns. That'll be enough to buy the salmon and the councillor.

V

A - I was madly in love with her; I nearly died of grief.

B - Died of grief! But you'd had her, hadn't you?

A - Yes.

B - And she loved you?

A - Passionately; and she nearly died of grief too.

B - Then how could you possibly die of grief?

A - She wanted me to marry her.

B - And what's the problem with that? A beautiful, rich young woman, with whom you were madly in love...?

A - That's true. But marriage... marriage... !

VI

A - I'd like to play some dirty trick on him.

B - But he's never done anything to you.

A - Someone's got to begin.

VII

A - I did what any sensible man would do when he's done something silly.

B - What's that?

A - I decided to put off being sensible till a bit later.

VIII

A - Madame de ... married a man of seventy-eight when she was still only a girl and he gave her five children.

B - Perhaps they weren't his.

A - I think they were; she hated them far too much for them to have been a lover's.

IX

Céline - He doesn't love me.

Damon - How could he? You're almost perfect in every respect.

Céline - So what?

Damon - Love likes to create its own image of perfection. It's impossible to idealise you; his imagination can't find anything to add to your attractions; it's been left in a vacuum.

X

Madame de *D*. - Who's that coming towards us?

Madame de *C*. - Madame de Ber....

Madame de *D*. - Do you know her?

Madame de *C*. - What?! Don't you remember all the nasty remarks we made about her yesterday?

XI

(Discussing a man lacking in personality)

D - But he's very fond of Monsieur de *C*....

C - How does he know? Who told him?

XII

Monsieur de *B*. - Ah, my dearest, we're lost... Your husband knows all.

Madame de *L*. - How does he know? Has he found

one of our letters?

Monsieur de *B*. - Certainly not.

Madame de *L*. - Has someone been indiscreet? Has one of our friends been trying to cause trouble?

Monsieur de *B*. - No, it's not that.

Madame de *L*. - What is it then?

Monsieur de *B*. - Your husband called on me this morning to borrow fifty louis from me.

Madame de *L*. - And did you oblige?

Monsieur de *B*. - On the spot.

Madame de *L*. - Splendid! Then we've nothing to fear – he won't know anything now.

XIII

The Master - Ever since your wife died, you've been getting drunk every day, you scoundrel. Before that you were only drunk two or three times a week. You are to be remarried by the end of next week!

His Valet - Oh sir, do let me mourn her a little longer.

XIV

A - I think, sir, that you owe me ten thousand crowns.

B - May I please request you, sir, to adopt some other hypothesis?

XV

A - You've got too low an opinion of mankind; there are lots of good people in the world.

B - The devil can't be everywhere at once.

XVI

A - If you do that, I'll never forgive you.

B - Is that a promise?

XVII

A - You've every reason to complain about his ingratitude.

B - Why? You don't imagine that when I do a good deed, I haven't sense enough to do it for myself, do you?

XVIII

A - Can you imagine how M... could have been so unperturbed by that dreadful act that shocked us all so much?

B - He's no more shocked by other people's dreadful behaviour than by his own.

GLOSSARY

ACHILLES: the main leader of the Greeks in the Trojan War. To make him invulnerable, his mother had plunged him as a child into the Styx, holding him by the heel. He died of a wound from an arrow shot by Paris into this vulnerable spot in his heel.

ALEMBERT, Jean le Rond d', 1717-83: his first names came from that of the Paris church on whose steps Madame de Tencin (q.v.) deposited her illegitimate son shortly after his birth. A noted moral philosopher and mathematician, well-known in intellectual salons of the day, he is chiefly remembered as the first co-editor, with Diderot, of the *Encyclopédie*, of which he wrote the 'Discours Préliminaire', setting out its ambitious aims (see Introduction).

AUGEAS: King of Elis, a region southwest of Athens, had a vast herd of cattle. As the sixth of his twelve Labours, imposed on him for having, in a fit of madness, killed his wife and children, the Greek hero Herakles (Hercules) was ordered to clean out, in one day, the long accumulated filth of the Augean stables or cattle-sheds, which he did by diverting the river Alphaeus. The guillotine treatment turned out to be rather more drastic.

BACON, Francis, Viscount of Saint Albans, 1561-1626: lawyer, statesman and philosopher, author of essays and maxims, the innovative theorist of inductive methods of science which profoundly influenced all future scientific research.

BALZAC, Honoré 'de' (self-styled), 1799-1850: recognised generally as France's greatest novelist, combining a prodigious, at times visionary, imagination with meticulous documentary realism to create – in what he named *La Comédie humaine* (1842-48), grouped into various categories: 'Scènes de la vie parisienne', '...de la vie militaire', '...de la vie de campagne', 'Etudes philosophiques' and 'Etudes analytiques' – a vast fresco of French life from the Consulate (1799-1804) to the July Monarchy (1830-48). His analysis of marriage, *La Physiologie du Mariage*, most clearly reveals his debt to Chamfort.

BAYLE, Pierre, 1647-1706: philosopher and critic. His subtle and witty *Dictionnaire historique et critique*, drawing attention to particularly crass examples of fanaticism and credulity, led logically to the, at that time audacious, conclusion that good conduct was not dependent on religious beliefs, which, in fact, might prove a hindrance. Bayle greatly influenced Mandeville (q.v.), was admired by Shaftesbury (q.v.) and provided excellent ammunition for the *philosophes* Voltaire, d'Alembert, Diderot (qq.v.), and others.

BEAUMARCHAIS, Pierre-Augustin Caron de, 1733-99: a resourceful and versatile adventurer whose multifarious, often suspect, activities included giving harp lessons to Louis XV's daughters, varied financial speculations, political intrigue, acting as a secret-service agent as well as producing a luxurious edition of Voltaire's works. He was an accomplished amoral 'survivor', now mainly remembered for his two great socially satirical and exuberantly lively comedies *Le Barbier de Séville* (1775) and *Le Mariage de Figaro* (1784).

BECKETT, Samuel, 1906-89: dramatist, novelist and poet, born in Dublin, spent most of his life in Paris; he wrote both in French and English and is best known for his play *Waiting for Godot*.

BENTHAM, Jeremy, 1748-1832: the earliest British propounder of utilitarianism, notably in his *Introduction to the Principles of Morals and Legislation* (1789).

BOUFFLERS, Comtesse de, 1725-c.1800: an early protector of Rousseau until their quarrel; the long-standing mistress of the Prince de Conti (q.v.); an impassioned admirer of the philosopher David Hume (q.v.), whom she often used to entertain in her own private salon in the *Temple*[12]. She professed, often acidly, austere moral principles which she blatantly failed to practise.

BRANCAS, Marquis de, 1672-1750: diplomat and soldier, promoted to the rank of *Maréchal* in 1741.

CADMUS: founder of Thebes, the capital of Boeotia; his companions were being killed by a dragon which he slew and, on the advice of the goddess Athena, he planted its teeth which then sprang up as armed soldiers who fought together until five were left, with whose help Cadmus completed the foundation of the city.

CALONNE, Charles-Alexandre de, 1734-1802: a *Contrôleur-Général* of Finance, dismissed at the moment when, having earlier displayed ruinous prodigality and general incompetence, he was starting an attempt to reform the iniquitous taxation system. Reflection No. 257 is thought to refer to him.

CAMUS, 1913-60: Albert, born in Algeria, French author of novels, plays and political works. He shared Chamfort's feelings about the contradictions and absurdities of life and felt the need to attempt to understand and perhaps resolve them.

CASTOR and POLLUX: twin sons of Jupiter. Castor was mortal and when he was killed, on the pleading of the immortal Pollux, Jupiter turned them into the constellation of Gemini. As they alternated between the Elysian Fields and the Underworld, when one rose, the other set, so they could never meet.

CELINE, Louis-Ferdinand (pseudonym: L.F. Destouches), 1894-1961: a doctor and writer, now best known for his two major works *Voyage au bout de la nuit* (1932) (*Journey to the End of the Night*) and *Mort à crédit* (1936) (*Death on the Instalment Plan*), which offered a disgusted view of mankind, truculently expressed in an often obscene and inimitably slangy style, and made Céline the most original and probably most enduring French novelist of his century. In his later years he became a notorious anti-Semite.

CHATELET, Marquise du, 1706-49: devoted to an often ungrateful Voltaire with whom she had a long (but not continuous) liaison, frequently providing him with hospitality. Cultivated and intellectual, she translated and commented on Newton's *Principia Mathematica*.

CHOISEUL, Duc de, 1719-85: soldier, diplomat and statesman, a believer in constitutional monarchy, Minister of Foreign Affairs from 1759, dismissed in 1770 through the influence of Louis XV's mistress, Madame du Barry, and the Church.

CONNOLLY, Cyril (pseudonym: Palinurus), 1903-74: critic, editor and writer, best known for his nostalgically Francophile *The Unquiet Grave* (1944).

CONTI, Prince de, 1717-67: an enlightened member of a collateral branch of the Bourbons, a protector of Beaumarchais and Rousseau, ran a salon with Madame de Boufflers (q.v.) as hostess in the *Temple*[12], where the young Mozart once performed on the harpsichord.

DANTE, Alighieri, 1265-1321: poet, born in Florence, best known for his epic, *La Divina Commedia*, a vision of hell, purgatory and heaven; the first is the most widely read.

DIDEROT, Denis, 1713-84: novelist, brilliant innovative literary and dramatic critic, originator of French art criticism, first and chief editor of the *Encyclopédie*; a man of great emotionality, exuberant enthusiasms and universal curiosity, including the natural sciences; an atheist, determinist and materialist, with premonitions of evolutionism; in sum, the most revolutionary theorist of his age, though he opposed physical violence.

DIOGENES, 410-320 BC: a leader of the philosophical school of the Cynics, ascetic devotees of self-sufficiency who believed that virtuousness was the sole requirement to achieve happiness. Notable for their outspokenness and shameless conduct, they (translated into appropriately coarse modern idiom) 'couldn't give a shit'. In addition to the stick (to defend their independence), which, with ragged clothes, formed part of the Cynics' equipment, Diogenes (reputed to be content to live in a tub, which he carried about with him) was also seen in broad daylight, with a lamp, in search, he explained, of an honest man. When the renowned conqueror Alexander the Great asked him if he could help him in any way, his reported reply was: 'Yes, you can get out of the way, you're blocking the sun.'

DONNE, John, 1572-1631: born a Roman Catholic, converted to Anglicanism and eventually became Dean of St Paul's Cathedral, London. His sermons were copious and widely admired but today he is best known for his poetry, which covers a wide range of styles: devotional, elegiac, satirical and erotic.

DUCLOS, Charles-Pierre, 1704-72: moralist and memorialist, known for his blunt but witty conversation; a supporter, with reservations, of the *philosophes*; a friend of Rousseau; admired and supported by Louis XV's mistress, the cultivated Madame de Pompadour. Apart from a subtly perceptive *Considérations sur les mœurs de ce siècle* (1750), he was the author of two novels, *Histoire de Madame de Luz* (1741): a sad cautionary tale of the hazards of being excessively virtuous; and an amusing *Confessions du Comte de **** (1742): an ironical picaresque story of contemporary morals. Extremely popular in their time, they are important examples of the 'libertine' novel.

EUGENE, Prince of Savoy, 1663-1736: general of the Austrian forces of the Holy Roman Emperor (neither holy nor Roman nor an empire in Macaulay's acid phrase), he'd successfully fought the Turks and, with Marlborough at Blenheim and elsewhere, the French.

FONTENELLE, Bernard le Bovier, Sieur de, 1657-1757: erudite, witty, assiduous frequenter of many salons, a lady-killer and writer in many genres: satire, tragedy, dialogues (in Lucian's style), essayist on various literary and scientific topics, particularly astronomy, e.g. his *Entretiens sur la pluralité des mondes* (1686), emphasising the puniness of the earth in the vast universe and suggesting that life may well exist elsewhere. In general, a vigorous advocate of a scientific approach to everything, including religion; an entertaining and truly international precursor of the 18th-century Enlightenment; and a member of the Royal Society of London as well as of the French Academy.

FOX, Charles James, 1749-1806: statesman and politician, held office at various times as British Foreign Secretary.

HELVETIUS, Claude-Adrien, 1715-71: one of the most influential *philosophes*; for information on his treatise *De l'esprit* (1758), see the Introduction. His wife's salon was frequented by d'Alembert, d'Holbach, Duclos (qq.v.), Chamfort and many others.

HOLBACH, Baron d', 1723-89: a German who spent most of his life in Paris; one of the most radical *philosophes*, he was a jovial and generous host, notorious for his well-argued materialistic and atheistic philosophical treatise *Système de la nature* (1770), in which Diderot was said to have had a hand.

HORACE, 65-8 BC: a poet of satires, odes and epistles, full of good humour, good sense, worldly wisdom, with a love of independence, country life and refined pleasure, expressed in a verse always carefully controlled, varied and full of felicitous phrases which make him one of the greatest and certainly the most charming and widely read of Latin poets.

HUME, David, 1711-76: Scottish philosopher and historian. His major philosophical work, *A Treatise of Human Nature* (1739), was written in Paris; he generously helped Rousseau (q.v.) and, like Helvétius (q.v.), he saw the pursuit of pleasure and avoidance of pain as the main motives of human conduct (cf. Lucretius). He developed the empiricism of Locke (q.v.) into an extreme, anti-religious, scepticism: we have become accustomed to seeing certain results follow certain causes, but what guarantee have we, he asks, that this will always be so? Chamfort shared his suspicions of metaphysicians (v. Reflection No. 240).

IXION: tried to seduce Juno, one of Jupiter's many consorts, but the infinitely ingenious ruler of the gods foiled him by turning her into a cloud. Ixion was then banished to the Underworld and tied to an eternally revolving wheel.

JAMES, William, 1842-1910: born in New York, a psychologist and philosopher, an upholder of pragmatism – the view that the truth of any assertion should be assessed from its practical consequences and its relation to human interests (to include religious and psychic).

JEROME, Saint, c. 342-420: an ascetic Christian scholar, author of the Latin translation of the Old Testament and the complete version of the New Testament to form the Vulgate.

LA BRUYERE, Jean de, 1645-96: his *Caractères*, (final edition 1695) consists of maxims and moral observations, both general and specifically related to the society of his day, in which, in a terse, rapid, graphic and sardonic style, he attacks the vanity, envy, selfishness, insolence, cruelty and follies of the upper classes of society of the age; his deeply pessimistic picture of mankind usually takes the form of disguised, often ironically humorous, portraits of his contemporaries. He also gives a moving picture of the miserable existence of the poor whom this society lives by exploiting or ignoring.

LA FONTAINE, Jean de, 1621-95: best known for his verse fables, taken from many sources, including Ancient Greece, Ancient Rome, contemporary Italy and even India. They appeared in twelve books from 1658 to 1694. A great nature-lover, he brilliantly attributes human qualities of speech, thought and feeling to all kinds of animals, with a freshness and simplicity that charms children, a psychological moral subtlety that intrigues adults and an amazing, endlessly entertaining and inimitable ingeniosity of versification.

LA ROCHEFOUCAULD, Duc de, 1613-80: author of concise, finely polished *Maximes*; first published in 1666, later revised and republished with some of their bleak and rather merciless pessimism attenuated under feminine influence. Nevertheless they still retain the general thrust of attributing all human actions to conscious or unconscious self-love. Chamfort was influenced by but never accepted this simplified view of human nature, and the style of his own Reflections is far less formal.

LOCKE, John, 1632-1704: mathematician and philosopher, the father of British empiricism, the belief that experience must be the basis of any consideration of human knowledge; he exercised immense influence on the *philosophes*. He was a strong advocate of religious toleration; in the days immediately preceding his death Chamfort was reading Locke's seminal treatise, *The Reasonableness of Christianity* (1695), in which he attempts to separate fact from dogma.

LOUIS XV, 1710-74: King of France from 1715; his main concerns were hunting and (a common Bourbon characteristic) copulation; his mistress Madame de Pompadour, a cultivated but sexually somewhat frigid woman, found it stressful to keep up with his sexual demands. His choice of ministers was often unsound; during his reign, France lost her colonial possessions in North America and India to Britain.

LOUIS XVI, 1754-93: succeeded Louis XV as King in 1774. In 1770 he married the daughter of the Holy Roman Emperor, Marie-Antoinette, an inordinately extravagant woman whose excessively conservative political influence over him was, to say the least, unwise and ultimately proved disastrous; they were both guillotined in 1793.

LUCIAN, c.115-200: a Greek satirist, noted for his mordant wit and famous as the inventor of the satirical dialogues, brilliantly adopted by Chamfort in his 'Little Philosophical Dialogues'. Inclined to stoicism, Lucian, a believer in rational common sense, particularly decried humbug, credulity and superstition; Christians were an obvious target, amongst many others. Lucian, who also used fantastic tales as a vehicle for his ideas, influenced French writers as diverse as Rabelais and Voltaire, and English writers such as Shakespeare and Swift.

LUCRETIUS, 1st century BC: the author of the *De Rerum Natura*, a long philosophical poem expounding the scientific and moral beliefs of Epicurus: the world, including man, is made up of atoms of matter; since there is no such thing as an immortal soul, the main concern of the living must be to seek pleasure, not in hedonism or luxury but by avoiding pain and anxiety, and living in simple admiration of nature and her beauty.

LUXEMBOURG, *Maréchal de*, 1702-64: a distinguished soldier, a friend and protector of Rousseau whom he hosted at his country seat at Montmorency.

MANDEVILLE, Bernard, 1670-1733: born in Holland but long resident in England, best known for his *The Fable of the Bees*, subtitled *Private Vices, Publick Virtues* (final edition 1726), in which he paradoxically, but plausibly, argues that what are traditionally considered vices, e.g. pride, vanity, greed, etc., are valuable, even indispensable, for the continuing prosperity and advancement of any great nation.

MARAT, Jean Paul, 1743-93: French revolutionary politician, leader of the extreme left whose virulent articles in *La Voix du peuple* and public notices encouraged the Paris *Commune* to take justice into their own hands. Alarmed at the progress of the invading Austrian and Prussian armies, in September 1792 self-appointed *Commune* tribunals summarily tried and executed roughly half of the inmates of the Paris prisons – a brutal example of mob law.

MARLBOROUGH, 1st Duke of, 1650-1722: English military commander who won several victories over the French, notably at Blenheim and Ramillies, which brought him not only his dukedom but also a magnificent palace near Oxford.

MARTIAL, c.40-104: poet and epigrammatist, today remembered for his satirical comments on contemporary events and Roman society. He was a friend of fellow-Spaniard, the stoic Seneca (q.v.), and in the last years of his life he retreated to live quietly in his homeland.

MERIMEE, Prosper, 1803-70: French playwright, historian, archaeologist and, above all, novelist and short-story writer, best known today for his *Carmen*, which provided the subject of Bizet's opera. A friend of Stendhal (q.v.), with whom he shared an ironic sense of humour and a certain cynicism, concealing a barelyperceptible tenderness. His signet ring bore the very Chamfortian motto (in Greek): 'Remember to be mistrustful.'

MESMER, Franz Anton, 1734-1815: an Austrian physician who advocated a form of hypnotherapy which became known as mesmerism.

MIRABEAU, Comte de, 1749-91: a self-styled 'plebeian' politician whose oratorical gifts and bold enthusiasms made him an important and popular figure in the early years of the French Revolution; he was even elected President of the National Assembly. His early death is usually attributed to his dissolute way of life.

MOLIERE, (pseudonym of Jean Baptiste Poquelin), 1622-73: a dramatist in both prose and verse who turned comedy into high art by ridiculing idiosyncrasies and follies inherent in all human existence, as exemplified in the society of his own day: affectation of all sorts (pedantry, snobbery, preciosity), religious hypocrisy, hypochondria, the irrationality of love, the general complexity and foibles of human behaviour as well as those peculiar to particular professions – often lawyers and doctors, of course – all treated in a tone that can range from gentle amusement to rank farce. He is arguably the most universal comic genius of all time; it is significant that in his youth he was a disciple of the eminent Provençal mathematician, physicist and epicurean philosopher Gassendi (1592-1655).

MONTAIGNE, Michel de, 1533-92: the first essayist of the modern age was Chamfort's favourite moral philosopher. In his autobiographical *Essais* (Books I and II published in 1580, enlarged and revised with Book III in 1588), he moves from a Senecan style of stoicism to a more sceptical, eclectic, refined epicureanism, summed up in his final famous query: 'Que sçais-je?' ('What do I know?'); he believed that suspending judgement provides greater peace of mind and personal independence, and, like Chamfort, set little store by a dubious consistency of thought or behaviour.

MONTESQUIEU, Baron de la Brède et de, 1689-1755: his outstanding contribution to the legal and political thought of the Enlightenment was his insistence that analysis of the political and legal systems of any country must take into account their historical forms of government, their relationships with other nations, their climate, their natural temperament, and their economic situation; and that any such analysis must therefore always remain relative and can never be absolute. His main importance for Enlightenment political thought was his advocacy of the British constitutional principle of the separation of executive and judicial powers.

NIETZSCHE, Friedrich, 1844-1900: a moral and political philosopher and great admirer of Chamfort; he turns Chamfort's religious scepticism into the absolute assertion that God is dead and converts Chamfort's relative pessimism concerning human weakness and corrupt society into an absolute affirmation that all hitherto existing assumptions must be reversed ('the revaluation of all values') and the world must and will henceforth be led by a few 'free spirits' – not clearly defined.

ORLEANS, Philippe, Duc d', 1674-1723: nephew of Louis XIV, Regent from 1715-23 during the boyhood of Louis XV. He had great fun in leading the profligate reaction against the austere bigotry of the later years of his uncle's reign and showed signs of a more liberal interpretation of monarchy.

POPE, Alexander, 1688-1744: a satirical and philosophical poet; a master of the heroic couplet and of the concise epigram.

PROUST, Marcel, 1871-1922: in his profoundly influential mammoth novel (originally in thirteen volumes), *A La Recherche du temps perdu* (*In Search of Lost Time*), he explores the nature and power of memory, the influence of habit, and the nature of love, both heterosexual and homosexual. It is unsurprising that Chamfort's many reflections on love would have fascinated him.

PUSHKIN, Alexander Sergeyevich, 1799-1837: one of the greatest Russian poets, author of the verse novel *Eugene Onegin* (1828), which contains references to Chamfort, and of the historical tragedy *Boris Godunov* (1825), both of which are now best known as operas. His library contained works by Chamfort.

RABELAIS, François, c.1494-c.1553: a boisterous, scatological and satirical physician and early French humanist, the author of a series of books describing the comical and fantastic adventures of the giant Gargantua and his son Pantagruel. It is in the second book entitled *La Vie très horrifique du grand Gargantua* that Rabelais introduces his 'Abbaye de Thélème' in which anyone who has learned the tenets of basic human decency (regardless of religion) is invited to do what they like. Rabelais's works were condemned by the Church for his mockery of religious practices and education.

RACINE, Jean, 1639-99: dramatic poet, master of dramatic pathos; his most important tragedies, carefully respecting the unities of time, place and action and written in the 'classical' French twelve-syllable alexandrine, include *Andromaque*, *Phèdre* and *Bérénice*.

RICHELIEU, Duc de, 1696-1788: great-nephew of the Cardinal de Richelieu, Minister of Louis XIV. The duke was a courageous, often victorious, frequently foolhardy *maréchal* who had a great reputation as a most successful amorist. Today his chef may deserve greater fame: after the capture of Mahon, the capital of Minorca, he invented a new sauce and named it 'mahonnaise', now enjoyed worldwide as 'mayonnaise'.

ROUSSEAU, Jean-Jacques, 1712-78: Swiss-born moral, political and social philosopher, musical theorist and composer (he contributed the article on Music to the *Encyclopédie*). He believed in the natural goodness of man, corrupted by living in society. His treatise on education, *Emile* (1762), emphasises the development of the heart and the intelligence by gentle example and physical recreation, rather than by reading and strictly verbal teaching. Though highly influential, it is now generally agreed that excessive reliance on the principle that education must always be 'fun' can easily lead to abuse, and his view that education for girls should be confined to teaching them submission to males, with the chief aim of producing good, healthy mothers, is simply odious. His own children were not given the chance to benefit or suffer from his theories: he consigned them to orphanages, explaining that it was for their own good; he may well have been right. His bestselling novel *Julie ou la nouvelle Héloïse* beautifully expresses his love of the countryside and idealises country life, and his emotional concept of sublime love had a considerable impact on the succeeding generation of Romantics. His *Confessions* were outstandingly popular, setting new standards of outspokenness, but they were also often mendacious. He differed from most *philosophes* in being Christian, with belief in the existence of an immortal soul. A quarrelsome man, ungrateful to most of his kindly friends, including David Hume (q.v.), he finally became a notorious paranoiac. His influence on the French revolutionaries was immense, e.g. in *Du Contrat social* (1762) his assertion that 'Man is born free; and is everywhere in chains'.

SCHOPENHAUER, Artur, 1788-1850: a pessimistic and misogynistic German philosopher, so great an admirer of Chamfort that, while openly admitting many of his debts to his works, he also paid him the compliment of plagiarising them.

SENECA: there were two Senecas: Seneca the Elder, c.55 BC-c.40 AD, a Roman rhetorician and historian, and his son, Seneca the Younger, c.5 BC-c.65 AD, a tutor to Nero but whose stoic insistence on a firm distinction between good and evil and the practice of justice, fortitude and temperance proved uncongenial to the Emperor. Condemned to death, Seneca committed suicide.

SHAFTESBURY, 3rd Earl of, 1671-1713: a leading English deist, i.e. a believer in God (as opposed to an atheist) but not in a revealed religion such as Christianity. A high-minded moral philosopher and social reformer, he was derided by Mandeville (q.v.) for his failure to acknowledge the manifest shortcomings of human nature.

STENDHAL (pseudonym of Henri Beyle), 1783-1842: novelist and author of biographies and critical works on literature, art and music. His best-known novels are *Le Rouge et le noir* (1830) and the historical novel *La Chartreuse de Parme* (1839). He creates heroes who combine 18th-century rationalistic analysis with romantic passion, in revolt against, while intricately involved in, the society of their age. The analogy with Chamfort is plain and is particularly clear in his markedly ironic anti-clerical pseudo-autobiographies, one of which has the significant title *Souvenirs d'égotisme*.

SWIFT, Jonathan, 1667-1745: clergyman and satirist. Born in Dublin of English parentage (he disliked the Irish while disapproving of the way the English treated them). His internationally famous novel of fantastic adventures (cf. Mandeville), *Gulliver's Travels* is a scathing yet humorous indictment of humanity's unfailing ability to misuse the faculty of reason with which it has been endowed.

TALLEYRAND, Charles Maurice de, 1754-1838: an outstandingly gifted politician and diplomat with a fondness for wealth, power and women, he had a reputation for successful venality, corruption and treachery. Successively a bishop; a convinced and 'enlightened' revolutionary reformer; a supporter of Napoleon as Consul and Emperor, whom he then deserted; a brilliant representative of the restored Bourbon monarchy (which he'd helped to overthrow) at the Congress of Vienna; and finally a valued adviser to the Orleanist Louis-Philippe, who replaced the Bourbons after the 1830 Revolution. He clearly deserved his outstandingly successful career (which earned Napoleon's neat, biased and inadequate description of him as 'a piece of shit in a silk stocking'); a man of outstanding intelligence, wit and charm with every gift needed to be a great diplomat.

TANTALUS: condemned by his father Jupiter to eternal

punishment in the Underworld, where, afflicted with a raging thirst, he was forced to stand in a pool of water which receded each time he bent to drink it, with a bunch of fruit suspended overhead which was withdrawn whenever he tried to reach it. Various explanations have been given for the severity of his punishment: that he stole ambrosia and nectar, the food of the gods, to give to mortals; that he killed his son and served his flesh up as a meal to the gods; that he stole Jupiter's favourite dog; and, worst of all, that he tried to seduce Ganymede, not only the cupbearer of the gods but Jupiter's own favourite boy.

TENCIN, Marquise de, 1685-1749: after a most disreputable early life (including a spell in the Bastille suspected of murdering a lover), she became very rich by speculation during the Regency and set up a highly successful and cultivated intellectual salon, where Fontenelle, Montesquieu and Duclos (qq.v.) were often too be seen. See also ALEMBERT.

TURENNE, Vicomte de, 1611-75: France's greatest military commander in the reign of Louis XIV. His successes included conquering Alsace and he fought campaigns in Spain and Holland. Commanding forces during the Thirty Years War, he helped to bring about peace in the Treaty of Westphalia in 1648. He was killed by a cannonball in 1675. A simple, modest man, he owed his success to careful calculation.

VOLTAIRE (pseudonym of François Marie Arouet), 1694-1778: best known of all the contributors to the *Encyclopédie*, the embodiment of the Enlightenment, an extremely prolific writer of tragedies, comedies, satirical epigrams, philosophical poems, an epic poem and countless prose works, short tales, essays on philosophical, political and judicial topics as well as an historian.

A stay in England led to great admiration for constitutional monarchy, empiricism and deism. He showed a taste for elegance and luxury, and took full advantage of the great sexual freedom of his age. He had sound business sense as well as being a successful speculator, and died a very wealthy man. His life was marked by a constant antipathy to all forms of injustice, past or present. Renowned for his epigrammatic wit and gift of repartee, he remains today mainly known for his short story *Candide*, a satirical demolition of unthinking and complacent optimism, a tale of amused, unmitigated disaster, crowned with a rather implausibly pragmatic happy ending: *'Il faut cultiver notre jardin.''* ('We must cultivate our garden.'). For work, he suggests, consoles, fortifies and is a source not only of profit but also of pleasure, which should be the essential concerns of any man of sense.

NOTES

1 Greek Anthology: a collection, ranging from 700 BC to 100 AD of over six thousand verse epigrams, including epitaphs, reflections on life and death, on love and family life, nature poetry, poets and artists; some are humorous or satirical (doctors are the usual easy target). They often throw a charming and even touching light on homely details.

2 Farmer-General: farmers-general bought the right to collect and retain certain indirect taxes; they thus were usually able to become wealthy, as well as unpopular.

3 *Philosophes*: this is the term used by Chamfort (and retained in this text) specifically in the meaning of proponents of the rationalist Enlightenment, often contributors to the *Encyclopédie*.

4 *Livres*: originally worth one pound (*une livre*) of silver, it had

become steadily and vastly devalued (see No. 169 for a very rough idea of its real value in Chamfort's time).

5 The present anthologist has hoped to avoid this danger by discarding (sometimes rather reluctantly) any Reflections that are, for example, too directly repetitive, throw little extra light on the general thrust of Chamfort's thought, or give no fuller understanding of his personality or his times; names of purely contemporary interest have not been included; names of major significance are in the Glossary.

6 Caryatids: female figures used in pillars to support the upper part (the entablature) of classical buildings.

7 Bucephalus: Alexander the Great's favourite horse.

8 Pandemonium: the capital of Satan and his peers in Milton's *Paradise Lost*. The reference is to Book II, lines 777 to the end.

9 *Little houses*: these were built in the suburbs of Paris (usually the western suburbs) for the use of the aristocracy and richer bourgeoisie as discreet love nests for clandestine love affairs, contacts with prostitutes, sexual orgies, so as to avoid scandal; they were a well-known and widespread institution.

10 Matthew IV.9

11 Who it was: Diderot (q.v.) has been suggested.

12 *Temple*: originally a fortified monastery of the Knights Templars, with later splendid additional buildings for the Knights of Malta where, as Grand Prior, the Prince de Conti (q.v.) had his magnificent salon; a small private one was reserved for Madame de Boufflers (q.v.).

SELECT BIBLIOGRAPHY

After relative neglect and fragmentary consideration, Chamfort's life has at last been the subject of an excellent biography published in 1988 in the series *Les Hommes et l'histoire* (Editions Robert Laffont) by Claude Arnaud, to whom I offer my unreserved congratulations, gratitude and acknowledgement. His work also contains a number of Chamfort's hitherto unedited, or, at least, never re-edited maxims, anecdotes and dialogues.

For main texts, there is the five volume-complete edition of Chamfort's works published in 1824-25 by P. R. Anguis. The most thorough modern edition is the Garnier-Flammarion (Paris 1968) by Jean Dagen under the title *Produits de la civilisation perfectionnée: maximes et pensées, caractères et anecdotes et petits dialogues philosophiques*; it includes a preface, notes and superb indices: an essential source.

Criticism of Chamfort's works has been somewhat desultory in French and even more fragmentary in English but there is a thorough and informative study in the *Modern Language Review* (No. 79, 1979) by Christopher Todd on 'Chamfort and the Anecdote'. There is a stimulating and enlightening article by R. S. Ridgway: 'Camus's Favourite Moralist', in *Studies on Voltaire and the 18th Century* (No. 199, 1981). Unfortunately the excellent long study, in the same series, under the title 'Chamfort devant la posterité' (No. 247, 1986) by John Renwick is available only to readers of French. Camus's introduction to the *Livre de Poche* edition of Chamfort's maxims, etc. is, however, available in English translation.

The general reader wishing to know more about the life at the court of Louis XV, with which Chamfort was so intricately involved, needs, even now, to look no further than Nancy Mitford's lively and informative biography of Madame de Pompadour, first published by Hamish Hamilton in 1954.

TRANSLATIONS BY DOUGLAS PARMÉE INCLUDE:

La Double Méprise (A Slight Misunderstanding), Prosper
Mérimée – John Calder 1959
Unwiederbringlich (Beyond Recall), Theodor Fontane – OUP
World's Classics 1964
Les Pléiades (Sons of Kings), de Gobineau – OUP, The Oxford
Library of French Classics 1966
Effi Briest, Theodor Fontane – Penguin Classics 1967
La Seconde Guerre Mondiale (The Second World War), Henri
Michel – André Deutsch 1975 (co-awarded the Scott Montcrieff
Prize)
Das Vorbild (An Exemplary Life), Siegfried Lenz – Secker and
Warburg 1976 (American edition by Hill and Wang awarded
prize by PEN club in New York)
Bel-Ami, Guy de Maupassant – Penguin Classics 1975
La Terre (The Earth), Emile Zola – Penguin Classics 1980
L'Attaque du Moulin etc. (The Attack on the Mill and Other
Stories), OUP World's Classics 1984
L'Education sentimentale (A Sentimental Education), Gustave
Flaubert – OUP World's Classics 1989
Nana, Emile Zola – OUP World's Classics 1992
Les Liaisons dangereuses, Choderlos de Laclos – OUP World's
Classics 1995